12572

S13049

ABOUT THE AUT

G000123503

Peter Russell has taught driving and driving instructors
Government and Government agencies on the driving test and is a frequent broadcast
He is General Secretary of the Driving Instructors Association.

10 MAIN REASONS FOR FAILING THE DRIVING TEST – AND HOW TO AVOID THEM

10 MAIN REASONS FOR FAILING THE DRIVING TEST – AND HOW TO AVOID THEM

Peter Russell

General Secretary of the Driving Instructors Association

B L O O M S B U R Y

All rights reserved, no part of this publication may be reproduced, stored in a retrieval system, or transmitted by any means, electronic, mechanical, photocopying or otherwise, without the prior written permission of the Publisher.

Publisher's note
The information in this book was correct to the best of the author's and publisher's belief at the time of going to press. While no responsibility is accepted for errors and omissions, the author and publisher would welcome corrections and suggestion for inclusion in future editions
of this title.

First published in 1993
by Bloomsbury Publishing Limited
2 Soho Square, London W1V 5DE

The moral right of the author has been asserted

Copyright © Peter Russell 1993

A copy of the CIP entry for this book is available from the British Library

ISBN 0 7475 1628 6
Designed by Planet X
Typeset by Florencetype Ltd, Kewstoke, Avon
Printed by Clays Ltd, St Ives plc, Bungay, Suffolk

CONTENTS

INTRODUCTION

YOUR DRIVING TEST

More than 50 per cent of people who take their driving test fail for things which they normally do correctly, but fail to do properly whilst on their test. The reasons for this are not hard to find. Most people practise with their friends and instructors and attain a reasonable level of skill. But unfortunately, when they are sitting with the driving examiner, they let their nerves get the better of them, and don't perform as well as they should. Some pupils, perhaps 15 per cent of the total, take their test before they are ready. But the rest should be able to pass so long as they have confidence in their driving ability and know exactly what the driving examiner wants to see.

The purpose of this book is to take the myths out of the driving test and to enable you to demonstrate to the examiner that you really are competent to drive on your own whilst you gain the necessary experience to become a skilful driver.

The ten main reasons for failing the driving test are listed here in order of frequency:

1] Failure to steer correctly.
2] Failure to make proper use of gears.
3] Failure to move off safely, and under control.
4] Failure to judge speed correctly.
5] Failure to make correct use of the mirrors.
6] Failure to signal and act on traffic signals correctly.
7] Failure to approach crossroads and junctions at the correct speed and with proper observation.
8] Failure to negotiate right and left turnings correctly.
9] Failure to negotiate roundabouts and exercise lane discipline correctly.

10] Failure to reverse and turn in the road correctly.

Before going into these common faults in more detail, ask yourself the following questions. If you answer 'no' to any of them, then you are probably not yet ready to take your test.

Are you ready for your test?

Can you read a number plate at 20.5 metres?

Can you enter the car, and carry out all the procedures safely?

Can you carry out the pre-starting safety check?

Can you move off smoothly, exactly when it is safe, and in your own time?

Can you move off on a hill, up and down, and from half a car's length behind another vehicle?

Can you steer to follow a SAFETY LINE, easily and competently?

Can you brake smoothly, and bring the car to rest exactly where you want it to be?

Can you identify and explain the purpose of all the main controls of the car?

Can you identify and explain the purpose of all the minor controls of the car?

Can you select all the gears easily on the move, without taking your eyes away from the road ahead?

Can you increase and decrease speed and match each speed with the proper gear?

Can you stop quickly as in an emergency when asked to do so?

Can you carry out the full sequence of M-S-M and P-S-L and L-A-D for any hazard that may arise?

Can you turn left and right safely, both into, and out from, side roads?

Can you negotiate roundabouts correctly and safely, turning left, following the road ahead, and turning off to the right from them?

Can you approach and negotiate pedestrian crossings of all kinds safely and correctly?

Can you meet, overtake, and cross the path of other traffic safely?

Can you reverse around a left corner with accuracy, under control, and with proper observation?

Can you reverse around a right corner with accuracy, under control, and with proper observation?

Can you park in reverse gear to the left and to the right, between two cars, in a space less than two cars in length?

Can you turn your car round in the road, accurately, under control, and with proper observation?

Can you follow a set route without any need for instruction or correction from an instructor or supervising driver?

Could you cope successfully with a driving test without making any dangerous or serious errors?

What happens during the test

The object of the test is to ensure that candidates are well grounded in the basic principles of safe driving, and are sufficiently practised to show they are competent and considerate drivers who will not be a source of danger to themselves or other road users.

The route lasts for about 30–35 minutes and covers less than five miles.

There would normally be:
• One or two roundabouts.

• Two or three sets of traffic lights.

• Fifty or sixty junctions and crossroads. Not all of these are obvious, because some of them will involve continuing along a main road without turning.

Candidates must:
• Read a vehicle number plate at 20.5 metres.

• Start the engine; move away straight ahead, and at an angle (for example, from behind a parked car).

• Perform a hill start.

• Overtake, meet and cross the path of other vehicles safely.

• Turn right- and left-hand corners correctly.

• Stop the vehicle as in an emergency.

• Stop normally at appropriate parts of the road as required.

• Carry out two manoeuvres involving reverse gear from these options: reversing to the left, parking in reverse, and turning the vehicle in the road.

• Give appropriate signals clearly and unmistakeably.

• Act correctly and promptly on all signals given by traffic signs and traffic controllers, and take appropriate action on signs given by other road users.

One cause of failure in many cases is nerves. All candidates are nervous, but if you are too nervous, it is often a sign that you are not sure whether you can cope. It may be just as well if you do fail, because

---

Avoid looking nervous

• The best way to look confident is to feel confident. But you can only do this if you know that you can cope with everything that can happen during the test.
• If you can avoid looking nervous, you will feel less nervous too. The only reason you should feel worried is if you think you are not yet ready for the test.
• If you are not ready, then get some more practice in on the subjects in which you feel weakest.

---

you'll be even more nervous the first time you have to drive on your own.

What the examiner says in the test

The examiner has a set script for the test. You will find you are far less nervous if you know exactly what the examiner is going to say. Read it through to yourself so you are familiar with the form of words. Ask your instructor to use this script for practice tests. This is what you should expect:

'Will you lead the way to your vehicle, please.'

'Which is your vehicle, please?'

'Will you read the number of [this or that] car, please.'

'Follow the road ahead unless the traffic signs direct you otherwise, or unless I ask you to turn, which I'll do in good time.'

'Move off when you are ready, please.'

'Would you pull up on the left at a convenient place, please.'

(If there is any doubt, or the examiner needs to be more precise):

'Pull up along here, just before [this or that place], please.'

'Very shortly I shall ask you to stop as in an emergency. The signal will be like this.'

(The examiner demonstrates by tapping the windscreen lightly with a small notepad; at the same time he will say 'Stop'.)

'When I do that, stop immediately under full control, as though a child had run off the pavement.'

(Once this exercise has been completed successfully he will add):

'Thank you. I won't ask you to do that exercise again.'

Take the next road on the right/left, please.'

'At the end of the road turn right/left, please.'

(At the roundabout, the examiner will say one of three things):

- 'Take the next road off to the left, please.'
- 'Follow the road ahead, please.'
- 'Take the road leading off to the right, please.'

(The examiner will then choose any two from these three options for you to demonstrate):

- 'I should like you to reverse into this road

on the left. Drive past it and stop. Then back in and continue to drive in reverse gear for some distance. Keep reasonably close to the kerb.'

- 'I would like you to turn your car round to face the opposite way, using your forward and reverse gears. Try not to touch the kerb when you are turning.'

- 'Would you pull up on the left before you get to the next stationary vehicle, please. This is the reverse parking exercise.
  'Would you drive forward and stop alongside the car ahead. Try to keep the two bonnets level and parallel. Then reverse in and park reasonably close to and parallel with the kerb. Try to complete the exercise within about two car lengths of this vehicle.'

(The final exercises are moving off at an angle, and moving off on a hill.)

'Pull up on the left just before you get to the stationary vehicle, please. Leave enough room to move away.'

(This is followed by):

'Move off when you are ready, please.'

(When you are back at the test centre, the examiner will say):

'Now I should like to put a few questions on the Highway Code and other motoring matters.'
(Then comes the moment of truth):

'That's the end of the test and I'm pleased to tell you that you've passed,' *or* 'That's the end of the test — I'm sorry you haven't passed, but your driving hasn't reached the required standard.'

The driving test report

Driving examiners now have to give a detailed report on what happens in the test, including reasons for failure. The front of the report looks like this:

DIA DRIVING INSTRUCTORS ASSOCIATION

Driving Test Report

Centre _____

Date ___ / ___ / ___

Candidate's full name _____

Name of School (where known) _____

Particulars of vehicle **P C S**

Make _____
Type _____

Category ___

Reg Mark _____

Oral explanation offered   Yes ☐   No ☐

Oral explanation accepted   Yes ☐   No ☐

Time _____

---

1. Comply with the requirements of the eyesight test ☐

2. Know the Highway Code ☐

3. Take proper precautions before starting the engine ☐

4. Make proper use of:

accelerator ☐   clutch ☐   gears ☐

footbrake ☐   handbrake ☐   steering ☐

5. Move away:

safely ☐   under control ☐

6. Stop the vehicle in an emergency

promptly ☐   under control ☐   Making proper use of the front brake (m/c) ☐

7. Reverse into a limited opening to the right or left

under control ☐   with proper observation ☐

8. Turn in the road

under control ☐   with proper observation ☐

9. Reverse park

under control ☐   with proper observation ☐

10. (a) Make effective use of mirror(s) well before

signalling ☐   changing direction ☐   changing speed ☐

(b) Take effective rear observation well before (m/c)

signalling ☐   changing direction ☐   changing speed ☐

11. Give signals

where necessary ☐   correctly ☐   properly timed ☐

12. (a) Take correct and prompt action on all:

traffic signs ☐   road markings ☐   traffic lights ☐

(b) Take correct and prompt action on all signals by:

traffic controllers ☐   other road users ☐

13. Exercise proper care in the use of speed ☐

14. Follow behind another vehicle at a safe distance ☐

15. Make progress by:

driving at a speed appropriate to the road and traffic conditions ☐

avoiding undue hesitancy ☐

16. Act properly at road junctions with regard to:

speed on approach ☐   observation ☐

position before turning right ☐

position before turning left ☐   cutting right hand corners ☐

17. Deal with other vehicles safely when:

overtaking ☐   meeting ☐   crossing their path ☐

18. Position the vehicle correctly:

during normal driving ☐   exercise lane discipline ☐

19. Allow adequate clearance to stationary vehicles ☐

20. Take appropriate action at pedestrian crossings ☐

21. Select a safe position for normal stops ☐

22. Show awareness and anticipation of the actions of:

other road users ☐

Examiner took action:

verbal ☐   physical ☐

Examiner's name _____

Examiner's signature _____

Authorised by the Secretary of State to conduct tests.

These are the sort of comments the examiner may make on the back of the report if you have failed:

Weather Conditions	Route No
Sunny after heavy rain; wet roads.	5

Brief Description of Candidate

Male, 17, well-built. Long hair in pony tail, blue suit and tie.

Remarks

④ Selected 3rd gear instead of 1st on many occasions. Stalled twice and was too slow moving off. Right turn into Brookside Road - candidate steered too soon.

⑯ Speed on approach too fast and emerged at Station Road without looking right.

D 10 No:	Code No:
Z 105301	M623

Disability Tests - Including eyesight failures

Driver Number															

Description of any adaptation fitted

Oral explanation comments:

REASON 1

FAILURE TO STEER CORRECTLY

DRIVING TEST REPORT

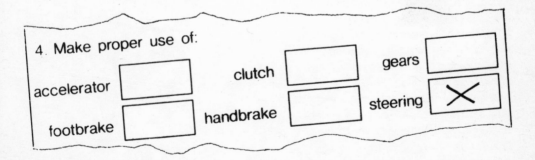

4. Make proper use of:

accelerator ☐ clutch ☐ gears ☐

footbrake ☐ handbrake ☐ steering ☒

Driving examiners have to write up their reports when they get back into the office. Those candidates who fail have all their serious and dangerous faults written about in detail. At the end of the test itself, the examiner will explain to you briefly why have you failed. In the office they go into more detail, and these are the sort of things they say:

What the driving examiner writes about steering

● *Candidate slow to take left lock off and mounted the kerb with the front nearside wheel when turning into East Street from Hill Lane.*

● *Candidate understeered on left turn from Beech Road into High Street, turning wide into it, causing oncoming traffic to brake sharply to avoid collision.*

● *Candidate kept one hand on the gear lever and then took both hands off the wheel allowing it to spin back after turning.*

Using the steering wheel

Hold the wheel lightly with your hands in the position of the figures 10 and 2 on the clock. This is called the 10–2 position.

Remember the examiner is looking for what is known as the 'white knuckle syndrome'. This means he can see you are under stress. Some examiners and instructors know too that white knuckles are a sign that you can't hear what they are saying. If they see white knuckles their feet creep closer to the dual controls.

The secret of easy and successful steering is to hold the wheel lightly but firmly in your fingertips, and always to look where you want to go.

When you are driving straight ahead you must always have both hands on the wheel unless you need to remove one of them to signal or change gear. Even when signalling or using the windscreen wipers you should be able to operate them without removing your hands from the wheel. This is worth practising.

The steering wheel is turned from side to side by making each hand move it halfway at a time. Hold the steering wheel with both hands, each in a comfortable position.

If you want to steer to the left you pull the wheel down with your left hand, and then push it up further with the right hand. To steer to the right you pull it down with the right hand and then turn it further by pushing it up with the left.

Having turned a corner you need to turn the wheel back again so that your hands are back in the straight ahead position.

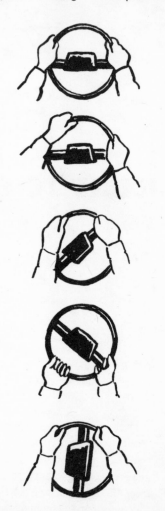

The correct position of the hands when turning left

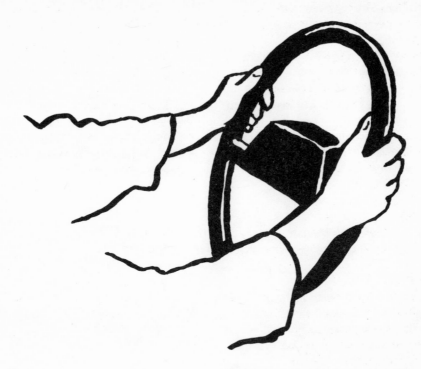

Always remember the 10-2 position

Steering properly

All learner drivers learn that crossing their hands on the steering wheel means auto-matic failure. This is not true, although learners who do cross their hands often fail. Crossing your hands is unnecessary, and you may end up with your hands in the wrong place when turning the wheel.

 Proper use of steering refers to what the front wheels are doing in relation to the road and means making sure that the car moves in exactly the direction that you want it to. If you practise properly you can improve your steering, and by the time you are ready for your test you should be quite good at it. However, positioning errors may take a lot more understanding to cure.

Practising
The best way to practise your steering is to sit in the car in a car park, or other empty space, and to practise turning the wheel from side to side – that is full lock left and full lock right – whilst keeping your speed as slow as possible. This way you will soon discover how easy it is to control your car, and to position it exactly where you want it. Ideal places to practise would include a pair of lamp posts, or large cones around which you can drive in a figure of eight, steering first to the right, and then to the left.

 Initially you will find that steering to the right is easier, because you can see pre-cisely where you are; but eventually you will have enough confidence to know exactly what sort of gap you have on your left-hand side, and how much room there is alongside you.

One thing you need to avoid is looking at the kerb and lining it up with the nearside headlamp, or the bonnet, when you are driving in traffic. Although it is comforting to have a guideline to make sure you are about 1 metre (3 feet) from the kerb, it is essential once you once you are driving to keep your eyes looking ahead.

Basic rules for steering

Successful steering relies upon a series of basic rules which apply regardless of the traffic conditions:

• First of all put your hands in the correct position on the steering wheel. You need to hold it lightly, but firmly enough to sense the road through your fingertips.

The next most important thing about steering is what you do with your eyes:

• You need to aim high. Look far enough ahead to plan your driving properly. Don't be taken by surprise by other traffic and road users.

• Look all round. Although you need to look well ahead, you also need to keep adjusting your field of vision to take in the broad view to your left and right.

• Above all, keep your eyes moving. Perhaps the one thing that separates learner drivers from those who have passed their tests is the ability to relax both physically and mentally. Don't stare into the distance at all. Make sure you take in the whole of what is happening ahead of you.

• Look ahead to where you intend to be in 5 seconds' time.

• See what is ahead of you that may change suddenly.

• Observe what may cause you to make changes to your speed or position.

• Work out how best to make those changes both smoothly and gently.

REMEMBER

• Place your hands correctly on the wheel.
• Keep your steering movements smooth.
• Turn the wheel at the correct time.

DO NOT

• Cross your hands on the wheel.
• Allow the wheel to spin back.
• Rest your elbow on the window.
• Take both hands off the wheel at any time.

! What can go wrong

• You may lose control of your steering by not keeping your hands properly positioned on the wheel. Remember the 10–2 position.

• You may fail to follow a steady course. Remember the safety line 1 metre from anything on the left.

• You may start to steer too soon or too late into a corner. Remember to plan your speed on approach to allow plenty of time.

• You may fail to turn the wheel completely from lock to lock when it is needed. Remember to practise this in car parks. And always turn the wheel as much as you need, not as little as you can.

• You may take both hands off the wheel completely. Remember that you must always have at least one hand on the steering wheel, and that you should have two on it unless you are using one hand to change gear or have one on the handbrake.

✗ You must avoid

• Turning the wheel too soon on corners. You might rub against the kerb or even drag the rear wheels over it.

• Swinging out on left turns. You could easily frighten another road user.

• Steering for any length of time with only one hand, or worse still, no hands.

• Crossing your hands. This won't fail you, but it may cause you to lose control of your steering altogether – and that *will* fail you.

• Allowing the steering wheel to spin through your hands. If you hit an obstruction you'll lose control of your steering.

• Keeping your elbow on the windowsill or resting your left hand on the gear lever when you are not actually changing gear.

TEST TIPS ✔

• There are only two things you have to control: your position and your speed. Your position is controlled by the steering wheel, and your speed by the accelerator, the gears and the brakes.

• The steering wheel is so important that you have to keep both hands in the correct position at all times. The safest way to hold the wheel is lightly, with both hands, at the 10–2 position.

• The steering is affected by your speed. The slower you are travelling the more you have to turn the wheel, and the more time you have to do so.

• The steering wheel affects the front wheels only, and causes the car to turn to the left or right. If you leave the steering wheel alone the car will keep going in a straight line. The faster you are travelling the more dramatic an effect the steering has.

REASON 2

FAILURE TO MAKE PROPER USE OF GEARS

DRIVING TEST REPORT

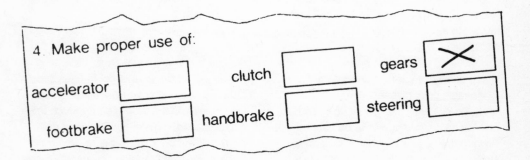

4. Make proper use of:

accelerator ☐　　clutch ☐　　gears ☒

footbrake ☐　　handbrake ☐　　steering ☐

What the driving examiner writes about use of gears

• Candidate did not use the opportunity to get into fourth or fifth gear throughout the drive, although we reached 30 mph on numerous occasions.

• *Candidate constantly looked down at the gear lever, lost control of her steering, and drifted into kerb or oncoming traffic.*

• *Candidate coasted into and around the corner when leaving High Street to enter Hill Road. And again when leaving Bank Street for Mill Avenue. Both occasions were dangerous and out of control.*

Proper use of gears

When examiners criticise the use of the gears, they are not nitpicking about the way you hold the gear lever or fail to palm it smoothly from one gear to another. They are talking about the use of the gears themselves.

What gears do

Do you know what gears do? Have you ever ridden a bike with lots of gears? The present trend for mountain bikes with ten, or twenty, or even more, gears on them gives you a very good idea of how gears work – if you let them. The reason we have gears on motor cars is so that the engine is not struggling to pull you away on hills, nor is it racing like a sewing machine at high speed. So at low speeds where you have to start to move the weight of the car, you use a very low gear, usually first. Then you should move through the gears as smoothly and briskly as you can until you get to a reasonable driving speed.

The gears help you to pick up speed, and to control your speed when you are slowing down. Second gear is ideal for turning into left and right corners; third is good for roundabouts, and also when you need to pick up speed quickly. Fourth gear is useful for town driving when you can't quite get up to 30 miles an hour. Top gear in most cars these days is fifth gear,

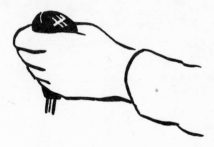

The skill of changing gear is to place your hand in the correct position so that you never select the wrong gear. Your hand should always push lightly in the right direction. Never grab the lever

though some smaller ones still only have four. Top gear is special, and you ought to get into it whenever you can. The reason for this is that top gear is not really a gear at all, but a direct drive from the engine to the wheels. All the other gears reduce the engine speed to make it slower and more powerful. But once the car is moving quite quickly, you don't need the gears any more and should get into top gear as soon as you can.

As a guide think of each gear as having a special role, and being best suited to a definite speed range:

• **First gear** is ideal from 0 to 10 mph, and you use it for normal starting, and for leaving awkward junctions.

• **Second gear** can cope with speeds as slow as 3 mph and takes you up to 20 mph. Above this speed the engine would be racing too fast. Second is useful for entering side roads, and tight traffic conditions.

• **Third gear** can cope with speeds from 12 up to 60 mph or more. It is best suited to picking up speed and coping with roundabouts and bends in country roads.

• **Fourth gear**, when it is not top gear, is for normal town traffic, and is used for speed ranges from 20 to 70 mph.

• **Fifth gear**, or top gear, is the gear you get into when you've reached a steady speed. Ideally you should expect this gear to have a speed range of 30 mph to whatever is the maximum. It is often difficult to pick up speed in top gear at the lower end, and you would normally not get into fifth gear until you have reached a safe cruising speed.

Examiners rarely look at which gear you are in. They can 'hear' it quite clearly, and with practice and experience, you will too. If the engine is making a high-pitched scream, your engine speed is too high, and the gear that you are in is too low. If your

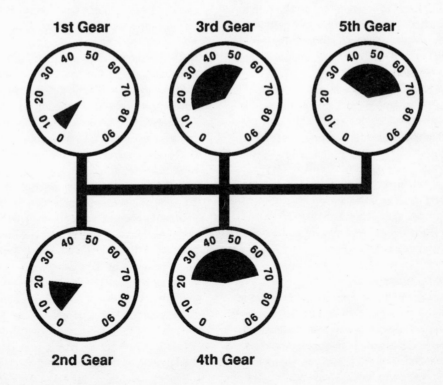

The speed range (mph) for each gear

engine is struggling at too low a speed, and is making low growling noises, then you are in too high a gear, and you will need to change down into a lower one.

It's all as easy as riding a bike; a mountain bike, that is.

Changing gear

The sequence for every gear change is also easy.

Get ready to put the clutch down, and put your right hand on the gear lever. Work out where you want the lever to go and place your palm correctly. If you grab the lever you won't know if it is going in the correct direction or not.

As you depress the clutch, take your right foot off the accelerator pedal and move the gear lever smoothly into the new gear. Then lift your left foot slowly from the clutch and press your right foot gently down again on the accelerator. Take your left hand off the gear lever and put it back on the steering wheel.

The skill is to make sure that you can do this every time without jerking the car. Do this by adjusting the engine speed to match the new gear you have just selected.

• If you are going down a gear you will need more acceleration.

• If you are going up a gear you will need less acceleration.

Using gears correctly

Remember that examiners are concerned about how you use the gears. They want to feel you select them smoothly. They want you to choose the right gear for the road conditions and the speed you are travelling. They also want you to change gear at the right time. The right time is easy to

work out, because it all fits into the ritual sequences of M-S-M (Mirror-Signal-Manoeuvre), P-S-L (Position-Speed-Look).

After you've looked in your mirrors and given your signal, you then carry out the manoeuvre. If you are slowing down, you brake or decelerate to the speed you want and then, only then, choose the gear you want. You might find that some older drivers have different ideas about changing gears. They will tell you to go down through the box, from fifth to fourth, then to third, and finally into second in order to approach a tight corner or junction. Modern thinking, and especially modern gearboxes, demand a more positive approach. Decide what speed you want to be driving at, and then select the most suitable gear for that speed. It's as easy as that, and saves a lot of valuable time when you are coming into a junction. Changing down from fourth gear straight into second is quite acceptable. You will not be failed for skipping gears.

Skipping gears when changing gear upwards is logical too, although you are not likely to skip gears as often. If you are picking up speed, make sure your gears are 'singing' to you before you select the next, higher gear.

One thing that all examiners hate is coasting, the deliberate selection of neutral in order to cope with a problem. There are two ways to coast: one is to select neutral, the other is to put down the clutch and keep it down. Both of them are wrong. Avoid coasting at all costs: coasting means you are not coping, and it would automatically be considered a potentially dangerous mistake.

Remember that both hands should be on the steering wheel for normal driving. Your left foot should be on the floor: don't keep it hovering over the clutch. Not only does this wear out the clutch bearing (and that can be expensive), it also tempts you to put your clutch down at the wrong moment. You never need to put your foot on the clutch until you know which gear you want next. Think positively about your gear selection.

Good early training with an experienced and qualified instructor can pay marvellous dividends. Smooth hand and foot co-ordination, coupled with recognition of which gear you need to be in for the next move you make, are the hallmarks of successful drivers.

Questions to ask yourself

Are you holding the gear lever properly?

• The examiner doesn't mind how you hold the gear lever. But if you hold it badly you could easily select the wrong gear.

Do you sometimes drive in the wrong gear?

• If you realise you are in the wrong gear, get into the proper gear as soon as you can. This fault won't fail you, but you might stall and then panic.

Should you select neutral whilst waiting to move off?

• You ought to select neutral if you have time whilst you are waiting at traffic lights. But don't stay in neutral for too long. Remember you need to be ready to move off when the car in front does, or when the traffic lights go green. If you are first in the queue get ready a little bit earlier. If there are plenty of cars in front of you, you can take your time.

! What can go wrong

• You may select the wrong gear. Remember to position your hand correctly; palm the gear lever smoothly.

• You may jerk the gears. Remember to use the clutch and accelerator in proper co-ordination with the gears every time, but especially when changing down.

• You may forget which gear you are in. Remember, it doesn't matter if you are in the wrong gear. If it screams at you, go up a gear; if it growls, go down instead.

• You may stall the car. Remember, the examiners don't mind if you stall. Then they can see if you do your starting drill again. Think why you stalled. If you were in the wrong gear, make sure you go back to neutral before you start again.

✗ You must avoid

• Taking your eyes off the road when you are changing gear.

• Coasting – that is, driving with the clutch pedal down, or worse still, driving in neutral.

• Holding on to the gear lever.

• Moving the gear lever before you know which gear you are going to select.

• Changing gear as you go round a corner or bend. (Select the gear you want before you get there.)

• Going through all the gears when you could easily miss out the intermediate ones when slowing down.

TEST TIPS ✔

- Make sure you have plenty of practice with your gear changing. If you are not sure of your gears you are not ready for your test.
- Make sure you can change gear easily and smoothly without any jerks.
- Know when to skip gears, especially when slowing down. Remember the rule: choose the speed, then select the gear.

Summary of Reasons 1 and 2

Control tricks to show off your skills
Accelerator Always make your acceleration smooth and controlled. A poor driver jerks the accelerator and doesn't drive smoothly.

Foot brake Similarly, when you are braking, keep it smooth. The faster you are travelling, the harder you will have to brake, but always taper off the brakes so that you prevent the bonnet from dipping as you stop. Remember the term 'bringing the car to rest', rather than stopping.
Practise this every time you pull in.

Clutch Avoid jerking the clutch. Avoid more than anything else the effects that are called 'Kangaroo Petrol'. This is caused by bringing up the clutch too sharply, followed by taking your foot off the accelerator, and then pressing the accelerator again.

Steering wheel Hold the wheel lightly. Remember the examiner is looking for what is known as the 'white knuckle syndrome'. This means he can see you are under stress. Some examiners and instructors too know that white knuckles are a sign that you can't hear what they are saying. If they see white knuckles their feet get closer to the dual controls.

Hand brake Never ratchet the hand brake. Although you will always hear it on television or in films, ratcheting the handbrake is an indication that you are too tense, or not thinking about what you are doing.

Gears The skill of changing gear is to place your hand in the correct position so that you never select the wrong gear. Make sure your hand goes around the lever so that it is always pushing lightly in the right direction. If you grab the lever you'll never know if it is going in the correct place or not.

The secret of showing off your control skills when driving is to be gentle, smooth and totally relaxed. If you are tense and hold everything too tightly you are bound to make the examiner worried.

The greatest single trick you use to show off your skill, of course, is that of ABSOLUTE CLUTCH CONTROL.

This means that *every* time you move off from rest the examiner sees that you do so exactly when you want to. You do this by showing that you can hold the car absolutely still on the clutch and accelerator with the handbrake released. The car does not move until the precise moment you want it to. There is no need to hold the car like this for long. A couple of seconds at the most is all that is needed. The examiner will be much happier about passing you once he has seen you do this every time you move off.

The controls of the car can best be remembered by splitting them into three groups: FEET, HANDS, EYES

The EYES are used by the driver to be sure it is safe whilst moving off, driving and stopping

The windscreen must always be kept clean; the mirrors must be adjusted to give the best possible view to the rear. What cannot be seen is hidden in the blind spots

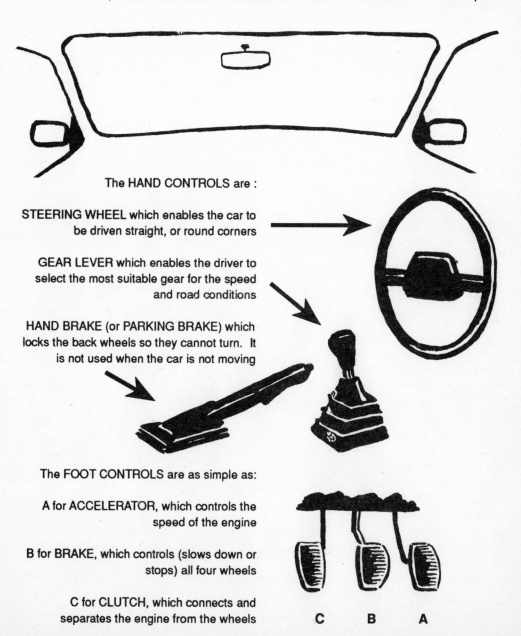

The HAND CONTROLS are :

STEERING WHEEL which enables the car to be driven straight, or round corners

GEAR LEVER which enables the driver to select the most suitable gear for the speed and road conditions

HAND BRAKE (or PARKING BRAKE) which locks the back wheels so they cannot turn. It is not used when the car is not moving

The FOOT CONTROLS are as simple as:

A for ACCELERATOR, which controls the speed of the engine

B for BRAKE, which controls (slows down or stops) all four wheels

C for CLUTCH, which connects and separates the engine from the wheels

C B A

REASON 3

FAILURE TO MOVE OFF SAFELY AND UNDER CONTROL

DRIVING TEST REPORT

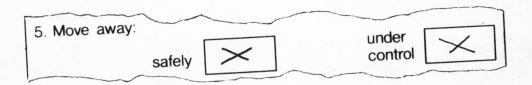

5. Move away:

safely ☒   under control ☒

What the driving examiner writes about failure to move off safely and under control

• Candidate pulled out into traffic without final blind-spot check. Caused an oncoming Volvo to brake and swerve.

• At White's Hill, candidate moved off but released handbrake too soon, causing car to roll back. Tried to stop on the clutch and stalled.

• Moved off with tyre screech at too high a speed. Candidate alarmed cyclist passing the other side.

Moving off

Moving off is simple, moving off under control needs more practice, and moving off safely needs the ability to join the traffic around you as quickly as possible and without causing it to brake or swerve to avoid you.

Moving off during the test

Most learner drivers are able to move off quite well by the time they take their driving test. However, once the test starts some of them begin to panic and stall. This is usually because they are unused to the examiner and the examiner's instructions. In fact, the examiner's wording is simple and fairly brief: 'Follow the road ahead unless the traffic signs direct you other-wise, or unless I ask you to turn, which I'll do in good time.'

What is meant is that you make all the decisions. This is the biggest difference between what you have come to expect from your instructor and the actual test. You now have to look for everything which affects you and take effective and prompt action on what you see. When the examin-er then says 'Move off when you are ready', the emphasis is on when *you* are ready.

You'll have to move off from the kerb on a number of occasions on the test, initially from outside the test centre. You need to be positive and confident in what you do: be brave, but not too eager.

The examiner will look to see if you observe to the front, then to the rear, and to see that you confirm the way is clear before you move out into the traffic flow.

The examiner will also check to see that you give the appropriate signals. This means giving a signal if someone else – anyone else – will benefit from it. But don't

signal if there is no one else around at all. Finally, the examiner needs to see that you move away smoothly and safely. This means getting up to the same speed as the traffic around you as soon as you can, so that no one else is made to slow down or wait for you.

The moving-off sequence

The sequence of moving off is always the same:

M-S-M and **P-S-L**.

Mirrors (and of course looking all round to cover the blind spots).

Signal if necessary. Indicators are usually sufficient, but you must remember to cancel them immediately after you've completed the exercise. Signalling by arm can be helpful, and is a useful way of showing how much control you have.

Manoeuvre The whole exercise is only completed when you've joined the stream of traffic. In other words, when you are in the correct **position** and driving at the proper **speed**. Provided you keep **looking** all round you will have fitted in the second half of the sequence as well: **P-S-L**.

The way you can demonstrate your absolute skill and mastery of moving off safely, and under control is as follows:

• Prepare the car for moving off. Select first gear, get the engine speed up just enough with the accelerator pedal, press in the button on the hand brake, and gently allow the clutch to take up the weight of the car. Signal if necessary.

Don't forget to check the blind spots before moving off

• Now make full observation. Look ahead, work out where you plan to be in a few seconds time. Look behind in the centre mirror, and in the door mirror. Then look over your shoulder to check the blind spots.

• If it is clear – and only when it is clear – release the hand brake and place your left hand on the steering wheel.

• Remove your right hand from the steering wheel and signal by arm that you are moving out. At the instant you have both hands back on the wheel, gently allow the clutch to come up further and gradually increase your engine speed to cope with moving off.

! What can go wrong

• You may stall. Remember to apply the hand brake or parking brake, and select neutral. Everyone stalls sometimes. Stalling will never fail you. Panic will.

Moving off safely

SAFETY POSITION (when stationary)

Door width 1 metre from kerb

SAFETY LINE

When your vehicle is in a parked position it should have its wheels about 15 cms (6 inches) from the kerb

As you move away from this SAFETY POSITION you will need to follow a SAFETY LINE which keeps the vehicle moving along a line which follows the kerb, but is about a car door's width (1 metre) away from the kerb or anything which is on your left-hand side

• You may have problems with your clutch control. Remember how to control the car, by listening to the engine note, feeling the bite on your clutch, and holding the car still before you move off.
• You may worry about holding up the traffic when you move off. Remember that if you have clutch control you can move off exactly when you want. But you must look over your shoulder to find out when it is clear.

• You may worry about the parked car in front. Remember the examiner would not have asked you to move off if it wasn't possible to do so. Use your steering quickly and your clutch control slowly.

✗ You must avoid

• Looking ahead when you should be looking over your shoulder.

• Getting too close to the car ahead by not steering soon enough or quickly enough.

• Stalling because you are too scared to use the accelerator and clutch properly.

• Waiting to be told to move off again.

• Asking which way to turn.

• Getting into the wrong lane.
• Failing to check your blind spots before moving off.

Moving off at an angle
The examiner will want you to move off several times during the test. Each time you do it, you need to carry out the same routine. On at least one occasion you will need to do what is known as the 'angled start'. This means moving away from

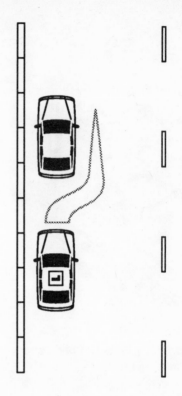

The angled start

behind another vehicle.
    The greatest requirement here is to know that you have absolute clutch control and that you can hold the car perfectly still whilst you look all round. When you do decide to move off you must turn the wheel quickly, but not allow the car to go too far forwards.
    The examiner will say: 'Pull up on the left just before you get to the stationary vehicle. Leave enough room to move away.' What he wants to see is just how good your clutch control and steering skills are. Moving off at an angle means you have to

look behind: you will need to demonstrate your confidence and show you are not put off by the car parked in front of you.

Always remember to check your blind spots.

What the examiner is really looking for when he says

Move off when you are ready please.

• Check that your cockpit drill has been carried out when you entered the car: door closed; seat properly adjusted; you can reach all the controls properly; seat belts are on; and mirrors are all properly adjusted.

Questions to ask yourself

What two safety checks must you make before you move off?

• Check that your hand brake is applied and that the gear lever is in neutral before you start the engine.

What does full observation mean when you move off?

• Look ahead to see the way is clear.

• Look in your mirrors (all of them) for any sign of movement.

• Look over your shoulder to check the blind spots.

• Look ahead to confirm it is still safe to move off.

How will other vehicles know you are waiting to move off?

• You must make eye contact with any other road user if you want him to wait for you.

Points to practise

Clutch control

The secret of safe and smooth moving off is always clutch control. With practice this will become second nature.

Clutch control is a matter of balance. You are allowing the power of the engine to replace the hand brake or parking brake. If you were suddenly to let the full engine power loose on the wheels of the car it would drive you forward about 10 feet in less than a second. For controlled moving off, this is how you can practise:

Start with the car facing up a very slight slope. If you take off the hand brake the car will start to roll gently backwards. So you have to keep your hand on the brake with the button pressed in. Now you can practise your skills with the pedals. Practise listening to the engine note change as your clutch comes up from the floor and you press gently on the accelerator. All of a sudden the engine starts to bite. At that point you must keep both of your feet absolutely still.

If you were to release the hand brake very gently now, one of three things would happen:

• The car could roll down the hill. If this happens apply the brake again quickly.

• The car could move forward. If this happens push the clutch very gently down – but only a fraction of an inch.

• The car could stay still, which means the engine power is not yet powerful enough to move you forward. You do, however, now have the car under control. If you now gently press on the accelerator and release the clutch you will move off smoothly.

Practise clutch control during your early lessons and you'll never worry about it again.

Once you have mastered moving off, you won't ever need to practise it again, though every time you move off you can make a positive effort to show that you have total control.

Moving off at an angle is the most critical clutch-controlled start you will do. You must demonstrate your complete control. This is simply a question of co-ordinating:

• Your feet on the accelerator and clutch.

• Your hands on the hand brake and steering wheel.

• Your eyes. Look all round to make sure the way is safe.

TEST TIPS ✔

• Look confident. Be positive.
• Carry out the safety checks, both on entering, and before switching on the engine.
• Select first gear, make full observation, including looking over your shoulder, and then move off. Join the traffic flow as soon as you can.

REASON 4

FAILURE TO JUDGE SPEED CORRECTLY

DRIVING TEST REPORT

| 15. Make progress by: | driving at a speed appropriate to the road and traffic conditions | ✗ |
| | avoiding undue hesitancy | ✗ |

What the driving examiner writes about making progress and hesitancy

• Candidate exceeded advisory speed limit (20 mph) through road works in Blythe Road.

• Candidate drove at excessive speed for conditions in Florida Road, with parked *cars on both sides and pedestrians near.*

• *Candidate applied hand brake, then went into first gear before making any observation at junctions.*

• *Candidate reluctant to pick up speed when normal progress could have been made.*

Judging your speed

One of the reasons why some learner drivers are reluctant to pick up speed during their driving test is that they are not very good at judging speed. All speeds are relative to what you know and learners are usually more used to judging speed either walking or cycling. Suddenly, you are travelling at 44 feet every second. In the time it takes to sneeze, you can cover the distance it takes to approach, pass through and clear the other side of a zebra crossing complete with zig-zag lines.

Distance and speed
Imagine a junction 50 metres away from you. If you are travelling at 30 mph you can cover that distance in three seconds (as opposed to 30 seconds if you're walking at 3 mph). You have a lot of decisions to make in a short space of time.

Consequently many learner drivers are reluctant to get up to 30 mph in the first place. Every time they think a decision is needed they like to give themselves a slight advantage by driving slower to start with.

This shows itself particularly when driving examiners are waiting to give the signal for an emergency-stop exercise. They brief the candidate about how the exercise will be carried out, and then wait for the candidate to pick up speed again.

They don't want to give the signal for the stop until the candidate has picked up speed, yet the candidate is reluctant knowing that any moment now, he will be forced to stop quickly.

You need to get used to looking much further ahead than you have previously done. As a pedestrian, you only need to look about five paces in front of you. As a cyclist you need to be even more conscious of what is ahead of you. Manhole covers, bad road surfaces, lumps and pot holes all need to be seen and avoided. Now that you are a driver you should also be more aware of the way that some cyclists dodge their way round obstructions without a thought to the vehicles behind them. At least learning to drive makes a better cyclist of you.

As a driver, however, you obviously need to cover much more ground in a shorter space of time. You need to make sure you have seen everything and can cope with it.

You cope by going slower when the need arises, not by going slowly all the time. Remember that you have the facility in a motor car to increase and decrease your speed quite easily by means of the brake or accelerator. Remember too: never change speed suddenly without using your mirrors first.

Keeping up with other traffic
The simple answer to learning to judge speed is to be aware of the need to keep up with other traffic. Get plenty of practice driving in both light and heavy traffic. You ought to be used to driving at speeds of up to 60 or 70 mph (depending on the national speed limit for the road you are currently on: 70 mph for dual carriageways, and 60 for single carriageways).

As part of your lessons on judgement of speed, and learning to cope with varying

Don't hold up streams of traffic by driving too slowly

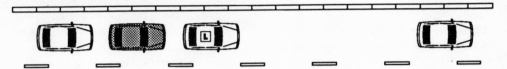

sorts of traffic and road conditions, you need to exercise care in the use of speed at all times. This means not going too fast, nor going too slowly. One way to measure how well you are doing is to compare the number of cars which overtake you in relation to the number which you overtake.

In your early lessons, you are not likely to overtake all that many. But as you get more experienced the number should even out. By the time that you take your driving test the number should be fairly equal.

Coupled with your judgement of speed should be your ability to make adequate progress, in other words to keep up with the flow of traffic. You are required by the examiner to drive at a speed which is appropriate to the prevailing road and traffic conditions. It is particularly important not to be too hesitant when you are emerging from junctions to join a busy stream of traffic.

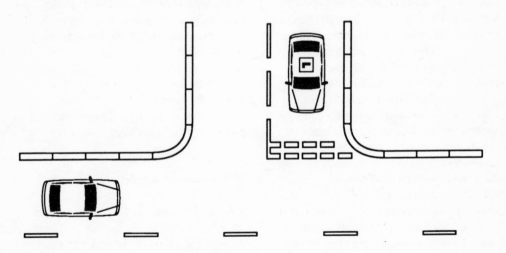

Don't hold up traffic behind you by staying so far back at a junction that you can't see when it's clear to go

Dealing with speed problems

Going too slowly
If drivers are not sufficiently experienced they find it difficult to keep up with other traffic. They are slow moving up through the gears, and hold up other traffic as a result.

The only real answer to this is practice, practice, and more practice, in order to gain more confidence in moving quickly and slickly through the gears; in using the accelerator pedal when moving off; and in joining and then keeping up with the traffic flow.

But you must remember not to over-compensate for this fault by driving too close to the vehicle in front, or at a speed which means that you cannot stop safely.

Stopping at junctions
Another fault is known as the 'junction stopper'. The driver comes to a junction, knowing that he is probably going to have to stop, and seeing little point in getting into a low gear, he stops, applies the hand brake, selects neutral, then looks to see what the traffic conditions are like.

The cure for this is to make sure you fully understand the sequence of approach to crossroads and junctions. As ever, the secret of successful safe driving is to make the correct decision at the correct time. This can only be done if you are fully aware of what is all around you before you reach the crossroad or junction, and at the same time have the control of the car so organised that you can carry out whichever decision you make easily and instantly.

Decisions really break down into a simple 'yes or no'. Or, more to the point, 'go or stop'. As you approach you need to plan your speed and control so that you can safely stop in comfort at any stage, or

you can continue to move forward slowly until it is safe to pick up speed again.

For example, if the hazard is a left turn into a busy road, you must plan with this in mind. You are likely to have to stop. The junction is controlled by a 'Give Way' sign. But 'Give Way' only means that. It does not mean 'Stop'.

When approaching both junctions and crossroads, it is of vital importance to check your mirror before slowing down.

! What can go wrong

• You may go too fast, but it is more likely that you will go too slowly. You need to show the examiner you can keep up with the rest of the traffic, but you ought not to be going any faster than other vehicles.

• You may find yourself stuck behind a stationary bus or truck. Remember that you may have to reverse a bit before you can pull out safely. But you shouldn't have got that close to start with.

• You may find yourself unable to see ahead. Remember, if you can't see, you can't decide when to go. Creep forward to give yourself a better sight line.

✗ You must avoid

• Holding up other traffic.

• Waiting at junctions, reluctant to move forward to see if the way is clear.

• Waiting anywhere where it would be safer to proceed.

• Interfering with the progress of other traffic.

• Being too cautious and not moving through the gears quickly enough.

• Failing to keep up with other traffic.

Making incorrect progress

• It is possible to fail the test for driving too fast, too slowly, and for driving at the same speed all the time.

• Try to plan your driving by looking ahead and working out when and how you can pick up speed. Your planning should tell you when to slow down as well.

• Try to avoid sudden changes of speed. These tell the examiner you haven't been planning properly.

REMEMBER

• **Proper use of speed** Drive within stopping distance and always maintain safe distance.

• **Avoid** sudden changes of speed or travelling too fast for the road surface.

• **Make progress** Keep up with other traffic subject to speed/safety limits.

• **Avoid** holding up traffic behind you especially when emerging. Wait where you can see clearly.

• **Anticipate** the actions of pedestrians, cyclists, motor-cyclists and drivers.

TEST TIPS ✔

• There is no special exercise during the test where the examiner is looking at your judgement of speed. This is tested all the way through.
• Try to show a positive approach to your speed. Look as if you want to make progress, and get round the route quickly.
• If the weather conditions are bad you can show you are aware of this by keeping a greater braking distance between you and the vehicles ahead. The same applies if the road surface or road conditions get worse. But don't fall into the trap of getting slower and slower.
• Drive at a steady speed, as close to the speed limit as the conditions allow.
• Finally, make sure you can stop safely in a distance you can see to

REASON 5

FAILURE TO MAKE CORRECT USE OF THE MIRRORS

DRIVING TEST REPORT

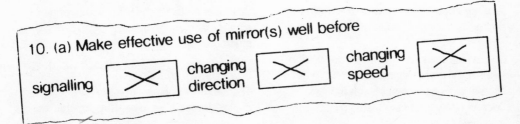

10. (a) Make effective use of mirror(s) well before

signalling ☒ changing direction ☒ ☒ changing speed ☒

What the driving examiner writes about use of mirrors

• Candidate failed to check mirrors before moving out for a right turn position when leaving High Street into Broad Lane.

• Candidate checked mirrors but ignored following vehicles and braked before signalling left.

• Candidate failed to use driver's door mirror before starting to turn right into West Street from Burgess Road. The motor-cyclist following was forced to swerve suddenly.

Use of mirrors

Some learner drivers fail their test and when they look at the item marked 'Mirrors' on the failure sheet, think: 'That's not right, I looked in my mirrors all the time.' But of course the marking sheet doesn't say anything about looking in your mirrors. It refers to making effective use of them, especially well before signalling, changing direction, and changing speed. There is the world of difference between simply looking into a mirror and taking action on what is seen.

Think of your mirror as your third eye

Always check that the mirror is adjusted correctly before you set off

Your mirrors are a vital part of your driving pattern. Driving examiners don't carry out a special exercise to test you on them, because they are being tested all through the driving test.

From the very first moment you move off you are expected to make full and proper use of them: you need to look behind you (and over your shoulder to cover the blind spots), and also to look in the two door mirrors. This is part of your 'Full observation' training.

This procedure is the first part of your M-S-M routine, and is an important part of

your normal driving along the road too. It is impossible to give an instant ruling as to how often you need to use your mirrors. Some instructors suggest you check them every 10 seconds, others say every 100 metres.

But the real answer is that it depends on what is happening around you.

For example, if you are driving down a busy high street, with parked cars, wandering pedestrians and a lot of following traffic, you will need to keep an eye on your mirrors almost as much as on what is ahead of you. On the other hand, when you are driving down a deserted motorway early in the morning, and the nearest vehicle is probably the truck you overtook 5 minutes ago, then you need only glance at much greater intervals.

Successful mirror use

The secret of successful mirror use is to make yourself a promise. Say that you will *never* be taken by surprise. If ever you find that someone has just overtaken you and you never even knew he was there, that is a black mark. Far better to think of every other road user as someone who will take advantage of you if you let them. What you really need to know is where every other road user is who could possibly influence what you are doing.

You must look out for road users who

might be travelling faster than you – they will want to overtake, so do your planning with them in mind. Others will be travelling more slowly than you, but when you have passed them they'll be of less interest to you. Those travelling at the same speed are the ones who will need special care when you are thinking about changing your speed.

• If you want to move off, look in your mirrors, look all round and go when it is safe.

• If you want to pick up speed, check in your mirrors that no one wants to overtake you.

• If you want to slow down, check in your mirrors and signal in plenty of time.

• If you want to change direction, check in your mirrors to see who is around you and whose path you may block.

It is not enough just to look in your mirrors because you want to do something. You need to keep in touch with all the traffic around you, and see how best you can help other drivers by noting what they are doing, and deciding what sort of signal they would appreciate from you.

Mirrors-Signal-Manoeuvre
Always use your mirrors if you are thinking of changing your direction or speed.

• Check what is behind you in the **mirrors.**

• Give a suitable, recognisable **signal**.

• Start your **manoeuvre**.

Build up good habits to keep you safe in years to come.

! What can go wrong

• You may be taken by surprise. Remember that not only must you use your mirrors, but you need to act properly on what you see. Look in your mirrors before you do anything.

• You may find someone overtaking you who you did not see. Remember that you still haven't failed. Make a conscious effort to look in your mirrors every few seconds.

• You may find you haven't left enough time to go round corners.   Remember, by .using your mirrors correctly you should have plenty of time to slow down. You will find that slowing down gives you time for everything.

• You may forget to look in your door mirrors. Remember that your two door mirrors are often called life savers. They will safeguard cyclists and motor-cyclists when you see them; and they might save your test too.

✗ You must avoid

• Not being aware of other traffic around you when you are manoeuvring. Always check your mirrors and blind spots.

• Looking in your mirrors but not acting sensibly and safely on what you have seen.

• Only using your centre mirror and forgetting the door (or wing mirrors) especially when moving to the left or right).

REMEMBER

- Your effective use of the mirrors is tested throughout the whole of the time you are driving. Consider the use of the mirrors as a third eye.
- The busier the traffic conditions the more you need to use your mirrors.
- You need to use your mirrors properly well before:
  - You move off.
  - You signal.
  - You change direction (especially if you are changing lanes).
  - You turn left or right.
  - You increase speed.
  - You slow down, especially when you are planning to stop.

TEST TIPS ✔

- Perhaps the best tip about mirrors is to ignore the advice that is so often put forward: that you should angle the mirror so that the examiner has to see your head moving when you look in it. This is not a good idea. Remember that the examiner is not so concerned about how often you look in the mirrors as what you do about what you see in them.
- Take action on what you see.

REASON 6

FAILURE TO SIGNAL AND ACT ON TRAFFIC SIGNALS CORRECTLY

DRIVING TEST REPORT

11. Give signals

where necessary ☒   correctly ☒   properly timed ☒

12. (a) Take correct and prompt action on all:

traffic signs ☒   road markings ☒   traffic lights ☒

(b) Take correct and prompt action on all signals by:

traffic controllers ☒   other road users ☒

What the driving examiner writes about signals

• *Candidate failed to signal left before leaving roundabout at Pycroft Hill, causing another car to change course.*

• *Candidate signalled too late before right turn. Motor-cyclist overtook.*

• *Indicator stayed on after left turn from roundabout and whilst driving down Peach Lane.*

Signalling and acting on traffic signs correctly

Situation control

When learner drivers first start their lessons they spend most of their time worrying about the car controls. Most of them think: 'If only I could master the clutch, or the gears, or moving off smoothly, all my driving problems would be solved.' In practice, once they do learn how to use the controls they discover that the real skill lies in 'situation control'.

Giving signals correctly is one way to convince the examiner that you have the situation under control. First of all, you need to remember that the examiner knows the test route extremely well, and is used to the problems that can arise. The examiner wants to know how you will react to them.

The purpose of any signal is to let other road users know what you intend to do. Good signals also help other road users to make up their minds about how they should respond to your actions. This is best achieved by getting the timing right. If you want to turn into a side road, make sure that the signal can be understood

easily. You have to be careful not to signal too soon, especially if there are any other turnings before the one you are taking. But on the other hand, signalling too late, after you have started your manoeuvre, can be just as bad – or dangerous.

Get plenty of practice at giving signals intelligently. One rule of thumb about whether a signal is needed or not is to ask yourself: 'Will anyone benefit?' Then: 'Can this possibly confuse anyone?' If it might be of help to anyone, including pedestrians, then you should give a signal. If someone could be confused, find a safer way to signal.

The correct sequence is, of course, Mirrors-Signal-Manoeuvre. For example, you see a woman walking towards a pedestrian crossing. She could easily beat you to it, and therefore you want to demonstrate your twin skills of situation control and vehicle control.

The best way to do this is to look in your mirrors. See who might be taken by surprise by your generosity in slowing down for the crossing. This means it is necessary to give the correct signal, 'I am slowing down', and to give it at the correct time. It needs to be seen by both the following and oncoming traffic, and also by the pedestrian who might want to use the crossing. Although the traffic behind can see and understand brake lights, there are two reasons why they are not enough for use at a pedestrian crossing. The most obvious one is that the pedestrians and the oncoming traffic won't see them. The second reason, especially applicable if you have a closely following car or motor bike, is that brake lights always say what you are doing, and not what you intend to do. If the vehicle behind is too close and you brake without warning, it may try to overtake you instead of slowing down with you.

Arm signals

The correct signal on approach in this situation, and certainly one which will earn you points from the examiner, is the arm signal. Your arm is fully extended out of the window and waved gently up and down. Signalling by arm has one tremendous advantage over other forms of signalling: you won't forget to cancel it after use!

The reason examiners like to see an occasional arm signal is that it demonstrates to them exactly how far ahead you are looking, how far ahead you can plan, and more than anything else, how much time you have to give clear, concise and helpful signals.

Thoughtful signalling

Thoughtful signalling is essential in any situation where others could be confused by your intentions. Changing lanes is an obvious example. Your approach to traffic lights and roundabouts is also likely to require careful signalling.

Remember, you can never be too careful as far as signalling is concerned. If you are taking a left filter at traffic lights, the lane may be signed 'Turn left only', but it is still not wrong to signal you want to stay in the left lane. Not all other drivers will be as watchful and aware as you are, so anything you can do to draw their attention to what you are about to do should be signalled.

Careless signalling helps no one, and can create dangerous situations, especially if the signal gives other road users a false impression of what you may be doing. One really dangerous signal that can fail you on your test is waving to a pedestrian whilst you are waiting at a crossing. NEVER wave a pedestrian across. You might think you are being helpful, but the examiner will disagree.

You know you are stopping for the crossing, but you can never be certain that anyone else will. Every signal must be confined to what you intend to do yourself. You should never try to signal to others about what they should do next.

Finally, remember that signals should only ever be given if they are part of your Mirrors-Signal-Manoeuvre routine.

Acting correctly on signals and road and traffic signs

During the test the examiner tells you that you are to follow the road ahead, unless traffic signs direct you otherwise. You need to look out for these throughout your test.

Road signs

You need to understand the basic principles of road signs, and then you will always understand what a sign means even if you have never seen it before.

Signs come in three basic shapes:

Circles

Circles are the most important because they give orders. Remember O for 'Orders'.

Red circles are prohibitory signs and tell you what you must not do. **Blue circles** are mandatory, and say what you must do.

Both must always be obeyed.

Perhaps the best example of how the system works is the sign of a bicycle. If you see a sign which is a red circle containing a black cycle it means NO CYCLING.

If a **blue circle** has a white cycle on it, it means this is FOR CYCLISTS ONLY.

Triangles

Red triangles are warnings. You are not compelled to do anything, simply look out for what is contained in the sign. So if a red triangle has a black cycle inside it, it means BEWARE OF CYCLISTS IN THIS AREA.

Rectangles

These come in an assortment of colours. But they all give information. If you see a rectangle containing a cycle you will know that cyclists are allowed to use this road, or should use the path specially designated for them.

Other signs

An **octagon** always contains the word STOP. Failing to come absolutely to rest at a white line governed by a 'Stop' sign could mean trouble for you - not just from your examiner but from the police as well.

The **upside-down triangle** has two functions. If it contains the words GIVE WAY, it means precisely that. You don't have any priority at this junction, and you must allow traffic on the main road to have right of way. If the upside-down triangle is empty it means that you can expect a 'Give Way' or 'Stop' sign in the next 100 metres or so. So you must still treat it as a warning.

Traffic lights

Traffic lights are fairly simple to understand. Everyone knows that **red** means STOP. You must not creep forward over the line whilst the red light is showing. But **amber** or **red** and **amber** together also mean STOP.

Green is the only traffic-light colour that means you may GO. But you may go only when you can see it is clear. If the road ahead is not clear then you still shouldn't move forward. Wait until it is safe.

Box junctions

Box junctions (look out for criss-cross yellow lines), were invented to indicate potentially dangerous situations. Unless you are turning right, you should never enter the box unless you can see that it is safe to drive straight through it without stopping. When turning right, you may wait in the box for the oncoming traffic to pass before completing your manoeuvre.

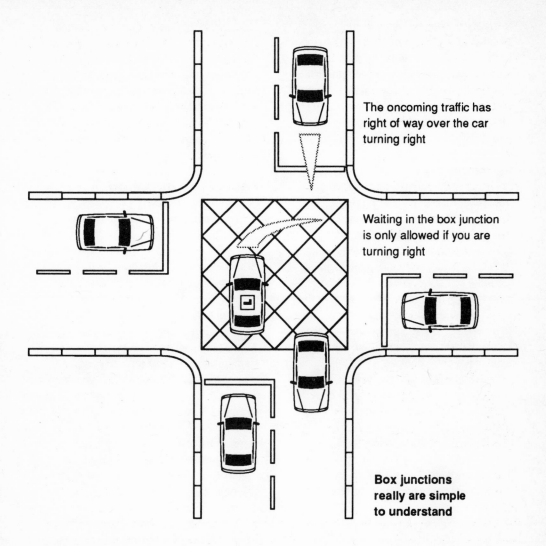

The oncoming traffic has right of way over the car turning right

Waiting in the box junction is only allowed if you are turning right

Box junctions really are simple to understand

Speed limit signs

Speed limit signs are also important and should be obeyed. Watch out for the new 20 mph limits. These are often used in busy, heavily pedestrianised areas, to keep speeds below the normal 30 mph allowed in built-up areas. Quite often 20 mph speed limits are found in areas where speed humps (sleeping policemen), bol-lards and paved areas are used to prevent traffic picking up speed.

Signals from other people

Finally, it is important to look out for signals given to you by other people. Sometimes signals will be given by policemen, traffic wardens, or lollipop patrols. Remember that these people have the legal authority to stop you whenever they wish, simply by pointing to you and putting up their hand, or their 'Stop' sign. Remember that stopping means actually coming to rest. Failing to stop will not only cause you to fail your test, but it can also result in prosecution and penalty points. Imagine explaining to your friends that you took your test to get your full licence, and lost your provisional one instead.

The other sorts of signals you will get are from other road users. Drivers, motor-cyclists, cyclists, people in charge of animals (including horse riders), and pedestrians can all signal to you. Not all of their signals can be found in the Highway Code. In fact some drivers are so out of date they still probably carry a whip in their car to wave. But the signals they give have to be understood and proper action taken by you if you are to stay in your driving examiner's good books.

Be extra careful with the elderly and the very young. Their signals may be confused. Look out for blind people and the partially sighted, and make every allowance for all other road users.

This is the signal given by an an authorised person for you to stop

Remember that road signs are put there for a purpose. Make a point of actively looking for road and traffic signs when you are practising your driving. As well as the signs already mentioned, don't forget white lines, yellow lines, directional arrows, and lane markings generally. These are all put there for a particular purpose: to make life easier and safer for all road users.

! What can go wrong

• You may forget to signal. Remember your M-S-M sequence.

• You may signal wrongly. If you do signal wrongly, one of the safest things to do is to go the way you have signalled, however irritating it may be for you.

• You may give an unwise signal. Remember, you can't tell other people what they should do; only what *you* hope to do. Don't wave people across at crossings, or drivers across junctions.

• You may confuse others by giving unclear signals. Signals are meant to assist other road users. Make them clear and obvious.

• You may give dangerous signals. If you signal that you are turning left into a road and then decide to go past the turning, someone could easily pull out in front of you.

• You may signal too late. If you brake first and then signal, the vehicles behind will get worried. The only safe sequence is M-S-M.

✗ You must avoid

- Giving a signal immediately the examiner tells you to turn. Remember the M-S-M sequence.

- Signalling too soon.

- Signalling too late.

- Giving signals without thinking.

- Giving misleading signals.

REMEMBER

- Your signals should tell other road users clearly and unmistakeably what you intend to do.

TEST TIPS ✔

- Giving clear signals to other road users such as pedestrians, not just other drivers, shows the examiner that you are in control of what you are doing.
- Good clear signals let other people know what you are going to do. Clear signals help keep traffic flowing.
- Make sure you cancel your indicators after us.

REASON 7

FAILURE TO APPROACH CROSSROADS AND JUNCTIONS AT THE CORRECT SPEED AND WITH PROPER OBSERVATION

DRIVING TEST REPORT

16. Act properly at road junctions with regard to:

speed on approach ☒

observation ☒

position before turning right ☐

position before turning left ☐

cutting right hand corners ☐

What the driving examiner writes about speed and observation

• *High Street junction with London Road, over crossroads: candidate had priority, but showed complete disregard for ambulance on right. Failed to slow down.*

• *Candidate didn't brake soon enough and approached Manor Road junction with South Street too fast. Heavy truck turning right into Manor Road forced to brake.*

• *Speed on approach to traffic lights in Baker Street too slow. Candidate missed green traffic light.*

• *Candidate failed to give enough clearance to cyclist before turning left.*

• *Candidate turned left into Park Street, failed to see that road was blocked.*

Approaching Crossroads and Junctions

You can pass or fail your driving test because of the way that you approach and cope with crossroads and junctions. The standard method of approach is the same that you apply to every hazard you will meet. The sequence is always the same: M-S-M, P-S-L, L-A-D.

These are very easy to remember, and you will need to say them to yourself many times in your early lessons. Make sure that you know what they mean, and how you apply them to every hazard you meet.

A hazard is anything which might make you think about changing your speed or direction. And nothing is more likely to make you change speed or direction than a crossroad or junction.

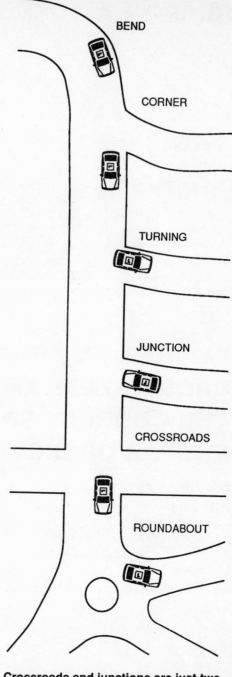

BEND

CORNER

TURNING

JUNCTION

CROSSROADS

ROUNDABOUT

Crossroads and junctions are just two of the'hazards' which may mean a change of speed or direction

• **M is for MIRRORS** Notice the plural: don't just rely on using your interior mirror, make use of the door mirrors as well.

• **S is for SIGNAL** Give the appropriate signal, using either your left or right indicator, to tell everyone around you what you hope to do.

• **M is for MANOEUVRE** The manoeuvre itself is split into three sections too:

• **P is for POSITION** If you are turning left, you should be correctly positioned anyway. If you are turning right, you need to get closer to the centre white line.

• **S is for SPEED** Adjusting your speed is the most important part of coping with any hazard. You can normally do this by braking. But if you are going uphill, simply

taking your foot off the accelerator might slow you down sufficiently. On the other hand, if you are driving fairly fast you will probably need to brake quite a lot.

• **L is for LOOK.**

• **A is for ASSESS.**

• **D is for DECIDE.**

As you look to see if your way is clear, you must assess the situation, and make your decision only when you have taken everything you see into account.

When approaching crossroads and junctions, if you have priority and everyone can see you have it – keep going.

If you have to give priority, take your time, arrive slowly and then make your decision where to wait and when to go.

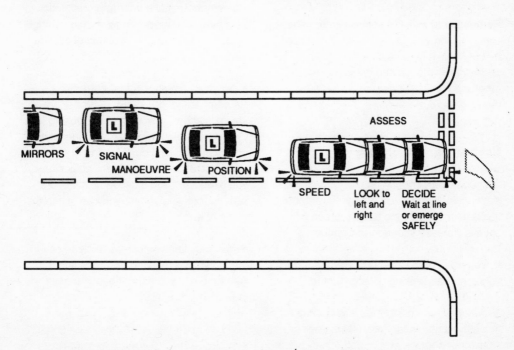

The sequence to remember when approaching crossroads and junctions

Normal driving consists of coping with a continuous series of simple decisions. Each decision is usually a choice between 'Yes or No' or 'Go or Stop'.

The decision can always be made by asking yourself a suitable question:

- WHAT do I intend to do?

- WHERE do I want to finish up?

- CAN I do it safely?

- WHO else needs to know? (**MIRRORS**)

- HOW can I tell them safely? (**SIGNAL**)

- IS it safe to proceed? (**MANOEUVRE**)

Remember to look out especially for vehicles catching you up; vehicles which may be overtaking; cyclists on either side; pedestrians who may be crossing; and any other road user who may be inconvenienced by your actions.

! What can go wrong

Speed on approach
- You may come in too slowly. Remember, if you go too slowly too soon you can always increase your speed slightly.

- You may come in too fast. Remember to brake sooner. Braking gives you time.

- You may run out of time. This is because you are coming in too fast. Remember to slow down sooner.

- You might not control your speed smoothly. Remember that braking is a skill. Taper your braking by being gentle at first, then firmer, and ease off the pressure at the end.

- You might need more time to look right and left. Remember, braking gives you time.

- You may stop too soon. Remember that stopping is only a help if you can't see that it is clear to move forward.

Observation on approach
- You may find yourself looking too soon. The difference that experience makes is in helping you to know where and when to look. Practise your timing on approach.

- You may find yourself looking too late. Remember to make your approach follow a safe pattern: mirrors, signal, brake, change gear, then start to look. Braking gives you more time.

- You may not plan ahead correctly. Remember that the secret of proper observation is knowing what you are looking for. On the approach to crossroads, junctions and roundabouts, your aim is to fit your vehicle into the traffic pattern. Look where you expect to be in 5 seconds' time, and plan your driving so that you can fit into the traffic flow.

- You may find you can't see clearly even though you've reached the white lines. Remember, if you cannot see you must creep forward until you can.

✗ You must avoid

• Approaching too fast – you'll not have time to see all you need to know before you arrive, and it will show.

• Approaching too slowly – you'll hold everyone up, and cause tailbacks.

• Stopping too soon so that you cannot see properly.

• Ignoring road markings telling you which lane you should be in.

• Failing to make a decision (to stop or go) at the correct time.

TEST TIPS ✔

• Use the M-S-M routine on every approach.
• Look for, and get into, the correct lane.
• Look out for any other road users who need to know where you are going. Keep a sharp eye open for cyclists who may sneak up on your inside.
• Give way to any pedestrians who may be crossing as you turn.

REMEMBER

• The correct use of mirrors; the correct use of signals; the correct use of brakes; and the correct use of gears on approach.
• The dangers of coasting (either by deliberately selecting neutral or by driving with the clutch pedal down).
• The need to take the correct safety-line approach through the corner.
• The need to give way to pedestrians who are crossing the road at the time, on either the road you are in, or the one into which you are turning.
• The dangers of turning in front of other traffic coming from the opposite direction, whether it is traffic coming from ahead driving straight on, or whether it is traffic which may be badly positioned in the road you are entering.
• The need for full observation at all times. Look for dangers from all quarters.
• The dangers associated with cutting right-hand corners.

REASON 8

FAILURE TO NEGOTIATE RIGHT AND LEFT TURNINGS CORRECTLY

DRIVING TEST REPORT

16. Act properly at road junctions with regard to:

speed on approach   ✗

observation   ✗

position before turning right   ✗

position before turning left   ✗

cutting right hand corners   ✗

What the driving examiner writes about positioning before turning

- *Candidate swung wide before left turn, crossed path of oncoming cyclist.*

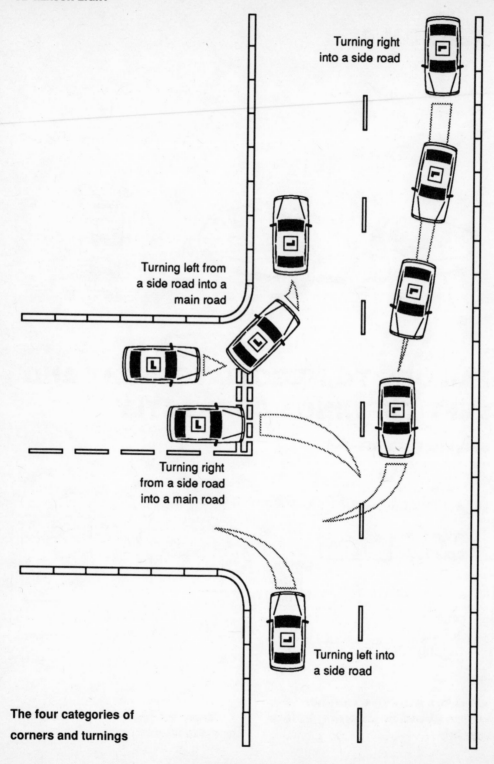

Turning right
into a side road

Turning left from
a side road into a
main road

Turning right
from a side road
into a main road

Turning left into
a side road

**The four categories of
corners and turnings**

• *Candidate cut corner when turning right off Avenue Road.*

• *Candidate went too far forward on right turn, clipped kerb with front wheel entering Acacia Avenue.*

Corners and turnings

There are four categories of corners and turnings:

• Turning left into a side road.

• Turning left from a side road into a main road.

• Turning right into a side road.

• Turning right from a side road into a main road.

The above are given in order of difficulty, the first category being the easiest.

Turning left into a side road means you need to keep your eyes open for traffic around the corner, otherwise you can expect to keep going.

Turning left from a side road into a main road means you have to look carefully to the right as you emerge, as well as to the left where you are going.

Turning right into a side road means taking extra care not to start your right turn too soon; make sure you can see into the side road, and be sure it is clear. But you also have to check that the traffic coming towards you won't be inconvenienced either.

Finally, turning right from a side road into a main road means you have to wait for everyone else. You have to be careful of traffic on your right and on your left as well

as anyone who might be turning into your road.

Correct sequence for turning

The purpose of M-S-M, P-S-L when applied to turnings is to make sure you start your sequence far enough back. The examiner tells you where you are to turn and you should start planning immediately. Use the mirrors, and see who behind you needs to be told what you are doing.

Give whatever signal is suitable. Usually an indicator is adequate. Signals by arm these days are not needed for normal driving test conditions, except for important slowing down signals when you want to tell a pedestrian you are slowing down for him.

There are three things to remember about signals:

• Give them in plenty of time.

• Make sure they are correct.

• Stop signalling as soon as the manoeuvre is completed.

If you are taking the second road on the left or right, make sure you don't signal too soon. It can be most embarrassing to fail your test because you were so keen to signal that you invited someone to turn into the road in front of you by wrongly signalling your intentions.

Adjust your speed first of all by decelerating. Slow down gently to start with, then brake more firmly if you need to, until you achieve the speed you want. Only then do you select the gear you want. As a general guide, you need first gear when turning out into a road, and second gear for turning into one.

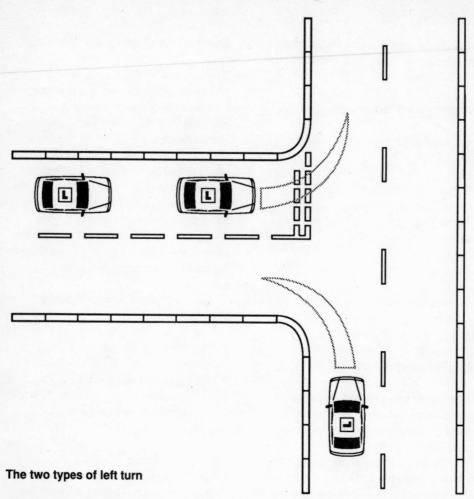

The two types of left turn

Approach to left turns

There are two types of left turn: each requires the same basic approach, but it is modified according to whether you are turning into a road or turning out from it.

The intitial approach is always the same:

M (Mirrors) Check to see who is following you.

S (Signal) Tell other road users you are turning left.

M (Manoeuvre) You should already be in the correct position. Brake, or slow down to the required speed. Then start to look all around (including mirrors again) to make sure it is safe to enter the new road.

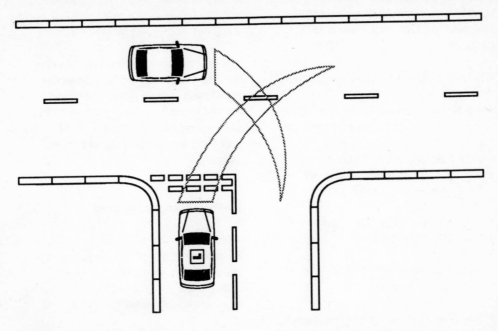

The two types of right turn

Approach to right turns
Right turns require the same basic approach as turning left with the additional concern of correct positioning. Always remember to avoid crossing the centre line or being too far from it. Take care also not to cut corners and to avoid turning in front of traffic approaching from the opposite direction.

Whether emerging out from a road or turning into one, you must ask yourself the same question: do you have priority over the traffic in the road you are joining? If not, or you are not sure, then go slower, and give way.

When emerging, choose the correct speed on approach, and then the gear to suit. Look to your right, and to the left, and to the right again. If necessary, keep on looking right and left until you have built up a perfect picture of the road you are turning into.

This is known as making **full observa-**tion. You can only make a safe decision if you are aware of everything around you.

• LOOK to both the right and the left.

• ASSESS the situation, by knowing who is there.

• DECIDE whether to keep going, or to stop.

Always carry out these sequences - the examiner will be looking out for your responses whenever he asks you to turn.

What the examiner is really looking for when he says: 'At the end of the road turn left please'

What two sequences should you follow?

● The two sequences are: Mirrors-Signal-Manoeuvre and Position-Speed-Look.

If you are already 1 metre from the kerb, and there is no one ahead of you, will you need to change your position?

● No. Your correct position for turning left is 1 metre from the kerb.

If the sign ahead reads GIVE WAY, must you stop at the white line?

● No. 'Give Way' means just that. Look to see if the road is clear, first of all to the right, then to the left, and finally to the right again to make sure it really is safe to keep moving. The sequence is Look-Assess-Decide.

If you are in third gear now, will you expect to change to a lower gear before you arrive at the junction?

● Yes. You would normally arrive at a junction in first or second gear, unless you know you must stop, in which case you can arrive in whichever gear is convenient.

On arrival at the junction should you be looking to the left or the right first?

● Look right first, except for very rare occasions, such as turning right into a one-way street.

If a pedestrian is waiting to cross the road *when you arrive, should you wave him across, wait for him to cross, or keep going if you can, but expect him to cross?*

● Never wave anyone across a crossing. Indicate that you are slowing down. You are allowed to keep going, but should allow the pedestrian to decide. Make sure you can stop safely, and still have time to use your mirrors and give a signal before stopping.

! What can go wrong

● You may swing out on left turns. Remember that most steering problems are caused by not turning the wheel enough: turn it fully and back again quickly and you should always get round.

● You may cut right corners. Remember that this is caused by turning too soon, usually because you are in a hurry.

● You may turn too late. Remember that this is usually caused by getting your timing wrong. Braking earlier gives you time.

● You may clip the corners when turning. Remember that this is caused by turning too soon and probably too gently. It can also be caused by being too close to the kerb when turning. Remember the safety line – 1 metre from the kerb for left turns; half a metre from the centre white line for right turns.

● You can run into the kerb, or across the centre white line, after you've turned. Remember that your position *after* the turn is governed by the position *before* the turn and the way you turn the wheel.

✗ You must avoid

● Not using all your mirrors.

● Not acting on what you see.

● Failing to signal clearly and intelligently.

● Not getting into the proper position for your turn.

● Ignoring white lines or traffic controllers.

● Failing to observe other traffic.

● Emerging unsafely.

● Stopping too soon, too late, or unnecessarily.

TEST TIPS ✔

● Look ahead and be sure you know exactly where you are going.
● Plan your sequence to give yourself plenty of time to decide.
● Mirrors, then signal, then position, adjust your speed, and start to look for any other road user who may affect what you want to do.
● Make your decision to go or wait.

REMEMBER

● The correct use of the Mirrors-Signal-Manoeuvre sequence.
● The correct regulation of speed on approach and use of gears.
● You must not coast on approach nor whilst turning.
● You must make effective observation before emerging, only emerging after giving due regard to approaching and other traffic.
● The correct positioning of the car before and after turning to the right.
● You must look out for pedestrians who are crossing the road at any part of the junction or crossroads.
● You must avoid turning in front of traffic approaching from the opposite direction when turning right.
● You must avoid cutting any corner when turning right.

REASON 9

FAILURE TO NEGOTIATE ROUNDABOUTS AND EXERCISE LANE DISCIPLINE CORRECTLY

DRIVING TEST REPORT

18. Position the vehicle correctly:

| during normal driving | ✗ | exercise lane discipline | ✗ |

What the driving examiner writes about failure to position the vehicle correctly

• Candidate changed lanes without looking whilst negotiating roundabout at Hill Lane. Cut across motorcyclist on left.

• Candidate straddled white lane line when approaching roundabout at Greyhound Inn. Following traffic confused.

• Candidate entered town centre gyratory system in left lane and kept in it even though we were leaving to the right. Cut *across following traffic as he changed lanes each time.*

Lane discipline

Basic rules

Keep left is the rule of the road. All you need to do for all normal driving is to remain about a door's width or 1 metre from the kerb or any hazard you are passing. This is the safety line which you are taught to follow in your first lesson on moving off.

You also need to avoid weaving in and out between parked cars. If you are passing a whole series of parked cars, and there are gaps between them that you could get into if you wished, how should you decide whether to or not? The answer is that if there is adequate room for oncoming traffic to pass you by without encroaching on the safety gap on your right, you should stay out. But if there is any danger that oncoming traffic could be closer than the gap on the left, you must move in.

If you want to show off your skills to the examiner in this respect, all you have to do is make sure that your timing is planned so that you are always near the kerb when oncoming traffic is passing, and that you pull out and pass stationary cars only when it is clear on your right. However, where lanes are specifically marked you must obey them. Watch out for and conform to any lane and positioning directions. This aspect of driving requires a lot of practice and concentration. In your early lessons your instructor will have made all these lane decisions for you. But as your driving test date gets closer, you will have to start making these yourself. If you cannot do so and you have less than two

weeks to go before your test, you need to think twice about taking it. Certainly, during the last five or ten lessons before your test, you should not require any help from your instructor in positioning your car correctly in relation to other traffic, or with regard to lane directions.

Make sure your instructor gives you plenty of pre-test practice, acting exactly as the examiner does, leaving you to make all your own decisions.

Where there are no lane markings, but you feel there should be, you will need to make positive decisions about where to position your vehicle. This is the sort of thing that makes the examiner realise how safe, courteous and considerate you are.

Roundabouts

Get plenty of practice at all you local roundabouts. Make sure that you know which lane goes in which direction, and ensure that you can always get in the one that is needed easily and in good time. Where local knowledge is essential you will find that examiners are quite helpful about giving you the directions. They will say, 'Take the road leaving off to the right, signposted Chester,' or perhaps, 'At the roundabout, follow the road ahead; that is the third exit.'

During the test

The examiner's instructions will be clear and concise. For example, he might say: 'At the roundabout, take the road leaving off to the right, please. That is the fifth exit,' or, 'At the roundabout, follow the road ahead, please. It is signposted Sutton and Town Centre.'

Roundabouts

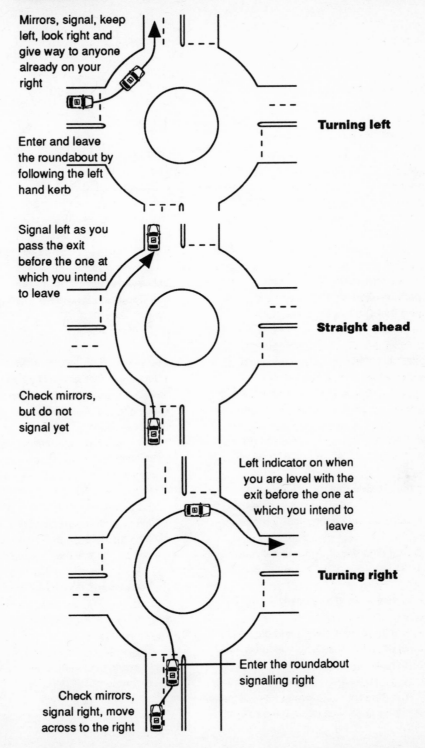

Mirrors, signal, keep
left, look right and
give way to anyone
already on your
right

Enter and leave
the roundabout by
following the left
hand kerb

Turning left

Signal left as you
pass the exit
before the one at
which you intend
to leave

Straight ahead

Check mirrors,
but do not
signal yet

Left indicator on when
you are level with the
exit before the one at
which you intend to
leave

Turning right

Check mirrors,
signal right, move
across to the right

Enter the roundabout
signalling right

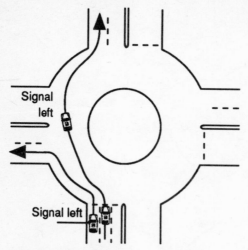

Three-lane roundabout - lane position and signals for turning left and going straight ahead

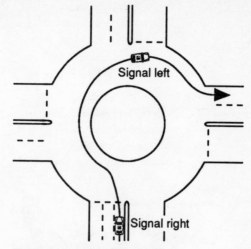

Three-lane roundabout - lane position and signals for turning right

The examiner will want to be sure that:

• The vehicle is under full control and in the correct gear.

• Road signs have been seen and obeyed.

• The M-S-M routine has been properly followed, and effective observation into and through the roundabout has been made.

• Due regard is shown to other road users.

! What can go wrong

• You may make inadequate observation on approach. Make sure you know where to look and when to look.

• You may get in the wrong lane. If there are lanes, you must get into the correct

one. If arrows or directions are shown you must stay in that lane all the time. If you have a choice of lanes, generally speaking keeping in the left lane is best.

• Large vehicles can't always fit into car-sized lanes. Allow plenty of room for them to manoeuvre, and don't overtake them when going round roundabouts.

• On roundabouts make sure you are in the left lane by the time you have passed the last exit before the one you want.

✗ You must avoid

• Approaching roundabouts too fast, or in the wrong lane.

• Changing lanes unnecessarily, or without regard to other traffic.

• Driving too slowly through large roundabouts, and holding up traffic on your right.

• Failing to use the door mirrors, especially the left one, before signalling to leave the roundabout.

• Failing to check blind spots when entering, or travelling around, large round-abouts.

TEST TIPS ✔

• Be positive as you approach roundabouts.
• Make sure you know which exit you want to take.
• If you are in the wrong lane it is better to continue in that lane and take the wrong exit if that is safer than trying to change lanes. You won't fail for going the wrong way. You *can* fail for cutting up other traffic.
• Get plenty of practice on all round-abouts in your area.

REASON 10

FAILURE TO REVERSE AND TURN IN THE ROAD CORRECTLY

DRIVING TEST REPORT

7. Reverse into a limited opening to the right or left

under control [✗]   with proper observation [✗]

8. Turn in the road

under control [✗]   with proper observation [✗]

9. Reverse park

under control [✗]   with proper observation [✗]

What the driving examiner writes about reversing and turning in the road

• *Reversing to the left* Reversing into St James Road, candidate steered late and drove across a white line.

• *Reversing to the left* Candidate failed to see oncoming car before the front swung out. Oncoming car forced to brake.

• *Turning in the road* Candidate failed to select reverse gear and car rolled into kerb.

• *Turning in the road* Candidate sat waiting for car to pass through whilst road was clear to continue manoeuvre.

• *Turning in the road* Candidate failed to see children playing on kerb until he had reversed too close to them.

• *Turning in the road* Candidate steered wrong way and finished up facing the same way.

• *Reverse parking* Candidate finished up wedged into the kerb. Tyres scraped against edge of kerb.

• *Reverse parking* Candidate failed to check in front before starting to swing out. Then failed to correct steering and finished at an angle.

Manoeuvring

Clutch control is not only the key to successful moving off, it also enables you to manoeuvre the car safely whenever you want to.

There are three set manoeuvres that you must be able to do safely and competently before you take your test. These are:

1 Reversing around a corner.

2 Turning in the road.

3 Reverse parking.

The three things which are needed for each of the manoeuvres are:

• Clutch control so that you can move the car slowly.

• Steering ability so that you can turn the wheels quickly to change direction.

• Awareness and consideration for all other road users.

You will be asked to perform two out of these three manoeuvres:

1] Reversing around a corner

In the test, the examiner asks you to pull up on the left, immediately prior to a left turn. Once you have stopped safely he will say:
   'I should like you to reverse into this road on the left. Drive past it and stop. Then back in and continue to drive in reverse gear for some distance. Keep reasonably close to the kerb.'
   What the examiner wants to see is what sort of control you can keep over your car whilst you are manoeuvring it at low speeds in reverse. You need to have excellent clutch control, an ability to work

out which way – and when – to turn the steering wheel. But above all you need to keep a careful eye open for all other road users. Full observation means just that.

Beware of
• Losing control of your steering.

• Causing danger or serious inconvenience to any other road users. This includes pedestrians who are crossing, children playing, and cyclists.

• Losing control by putting the clutch

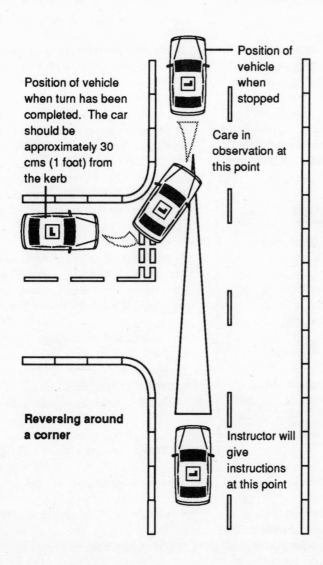

Position of vehicle when turn has been completed. The car should be approximately 30 cms (1 foot) from the kerb

Position of vehicle when stopped

Care in observation at this point

Reversing around a corner

Instructor will give instructions at this point

down too soon if going downhill.
* Steering too wide or into the kerb without correction.

* Not looking where you are going.

* Not checking the road is clear to the front before you start, and before your front swings out.

Minor errors which are acceptable include stalling, selecting the wrong gear (so long as you correct it immediately), and momentarily steering the wrong way.
Reversing is easy. Provided you can make the car go forward slowly and under full control, you should have no difficulty in doing the same backwards - with practice.

Rules for reversing

1 Control the speed on the clutch and accelerator when possible.

2 Make sure it is safe before moving.

3 Look where you are going.

4 If you may hinder anyone else, *stop*. Move forward if necessary and wait until it is safe before reversing again.

! What can go wrong

* You may forget to look round before swinging out. Remember that other traffic is travelling normally. You are the unusual one. Look all round to the front before you start the turn.

* You may forget which way to steer. Remember that the wheels face the same way regardless of whether you are going forwards or backwards. A left reverse is the same as a front left turn.

* You may oversteer on the turn. Remember that as soon as you are on full lock you ought to straighten up again.

* You may understeer and not get round. Remember that if you don't turn the steering wheel enough you will not get round a 90° corner.

* You may steer too soon. Remember to look through the rear side window to check the precise moment to start the turn.

* You may steer too late. Remember that turning too late will put you wide in the side road.

* You may find traffic coming towards you whilst you are reversing. Remember that you are the one who has to stop. If necessary, go forward and wait until it is clear.

* You may make a complete mess of the manoeuvre. Remember, you cannot ask the examiner if you can do the manoeuvre again; but you can do so without asking him. Just go forward and start again.

✗ You must avoid

* Steering too soon, or too late.

* Not looking all round before moving off.

* Losing clutch control or moving too fast.

* Not looking out for other road users.

TEST TIPS ✔

- Get comfortable in your seat first.
- Remove your seat belt if you wish.
- Look all around to see if the way is clear.
- Move off in reverse, slowly, looking behind you as you go.
- Look where you are going until you decide where to stop.

2] Turning in the road

This is often referred to as the **three-point turn**.

In the test the examiner asks you to pull up at a convenient place at the roadside, and says:

'I would like you to turn your car round to face the opposite way using forward and reverse gears. Try not to touch the kerb

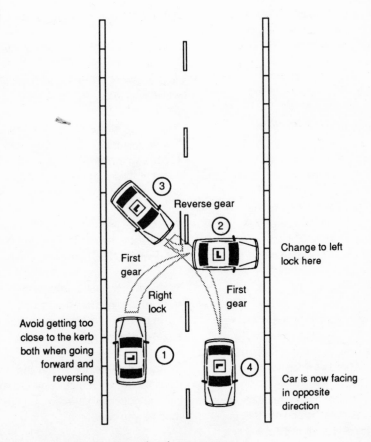

Turning in the road using forward and reverse gears

when you're turning.'

What he means is that he wants you to show him how well you can handle the car in a confined space and to see your judgement of the positioning of your car in relation to the kerb. What he is looking for is excellent clutch control and your co-ordination of the clutch with the accelerator and parking brake. He will also look to see if you know which way to turn the steering wheel, and how soon and how far to turn it. He also wants to see if you are aware of every other road user who might be affected by what you are doing, and how you react to them.

You need to select the safest spot, only move when it is safe, and manoeuvre efficiently and effectively. You should do it in three moves.

Beware of
• Mounting or bouncing into the kerb.

• Causing danger or serious inconvenience to other road users.

• Losing control of the car by not having proper clutch control, or repeatedly stalling.

• Not selecting the correct gear and rolling back.

Minor errors which are acceptable include stalling, selecting the wrong gear (but correcting the mistake), even steering the wrong way, provided you correct the fault immediately.

However, if you continue to get flustered whenever you are practising your turn in the road exercise you are still not ready to take your test.

REMEMBER

• The correct co-ordination of the accelerator with the footbrake and the clutch with the steering.
• The need for full and correct observation prior to each of the phases and whilst moving.
• The need to be reasonably accurate with the placement of the car at all times.

! What can go wrong

• You may forget which way to steer. Remember to hold the car under clutch control before you move while you think which way to go.

• You may choose a bad place to turn. Remember that the examiner asks you to choose where to stop. Look out for and avoid problems like lamp posts, trees, children playing, and gateways.

• You may find the road very busy. Remember, the examiner selects the road. If it doesn't clear, he'll move you on.

• You may block the road before you reverse. Remember that most people are not in a hurry, but if they are waiting for you to get out of their way, do so.

• You may get stuck on the camber. Remember that you don't need to go right into the gutter for your turn. Use as little road as you need.

• You may take too many turns. Remember you don't have to complete the manoeuvre in three moves. But you can help yourself by taking it slowly, and steering the wheel quickly.

• You might forget where to look next. Remember that observation is the greatest single skill that any driver can have.

✗ You must avoid

• Starting from a bad position.

• Not looking out for children playing or other obstructions.

• Losing clutch control or not remembering which way to turn the wheel.

TEST TIPS ✓

• Get comfortable first — then look all round for any traffic coming.
• Make your first movement very effective by steering quickly, but keep your speed slow by using clutch control.
• Full observation means looking for any traffic which may be impeded by your efforts. Wait if you can but if the other vehicles want you to continue, do so.

3] Parking in reverse gear

The examiner asks you to pull up at the kerbside, and says:

'Would you drive forward and stop alongside the car ahead. Try to keep the two bonnets level and parallel. Then reverse in and park reasonably close to and parallel with the kerb. Try to complete the exercise within about two car lengths of this vehicle.'

What he means is that he wants you to pretend you are reversing into a parking-meter bay (as you will have to do many times when you have passed your test). Examiners don't like you to risk parking between two cars, so they use only one. The examiner will look to see that you have good judgement of distance and width, and also of the intentions of other road users.

You could fail by:

• Losing control of your steering.

• Causing danger or serious inconvenience to other road users.

• Losing control of the clutch, accelerator or footbrake.

• Getting too close to the parked car.

• Not looking around to the front before you start.

• Not looking around to the front before you turn the wheels out.

• Not looking behind you – that is, where you are going – most of the time.

• Looking to the front when you are going backwards for any length of time.

Minor errors which are acceptable include stalling, steering the wrong way, and selecting the wrong gear (so long as you correct it immediately).

! What can go wrong

• You may start to steer too late. Remember that you should begin to turn your wheels as soon as the two cars are level. You can't hit the car alongside you.

• You may start to turn too soon. Remember that you need to turn as soon as your rear bumper is level with the bumper of the car alongside.

• You may start too close to the parked car. Remember that you ought to start parallel, about a door's width from it. If you are any closer, you are too close.

• You may turn the wrong way. Remember

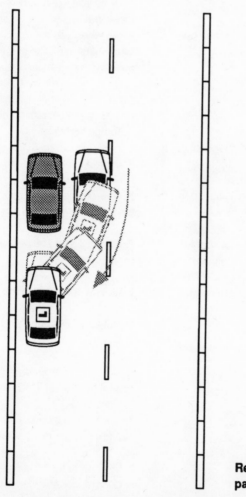

**Reversing into a
parking space**

that if you turn your wheel to the right instead of the left you will hit the parked car. Stop immediately, go forward and start again – properly.

• You may forget to look all round before you turn the wheel. Remember that oncoming traffic has priority. Look before you turn.

• You may reverse too far back. Remember that the examiner wants you to reverse no more than two car lengths. Keep well within this distance.

• You may hit the pavement. Remember, this indicates that you are reversing at too sharp an angle.

✗ You must avoid

• Getting too close to the parked car at the start.

• Starting to move off before it is clear.

• Not looking all round before you start to move.

• Commencing your turn too late, or not straightening up early enough.

• Not looking where you are going.

• Not looking all round before you swing out.

REMEMBER

• The correct co-ordination of the accelerator with the footbrake and the clutch, and with the steering.
• The need for full and correct observation prior to each of the stages of the reverse park, and whilst moving.
• The need to be reasonably accurate with the placement of the car at all times. The degree of skill you show will depend upon what stage you are at in learning to drive, and the road and traffic conditions which exist at the time.

TEST TIPS ✔

• Make sure you have had lots of practice.
• Start at least a door's width wider than the leading car.
• Have a good look all round before you start to move off.
• Reverse very slowly, under clutch control if you can.
• Look round again before you swing out.
• Look at the car – or gap – which is behind you to aim at.

CONCLUSION

THE REST OF THE TEST

Finally, here are some important tips to help you gain confidence before you take your test.

Check your car before you arrive

Apart from producing your driving licence, having your appointment card, and being able to read a number plate at 20.5 metres, you need to know that your car is suitable for the test. You should get your instructor to confirm each of the following for you:

● That the car is in good mechanical condition, with lights, indicators, windscreen wipers and washers, and horn all working.

● That L- plates and a current tax disc are displayed.

● That the bodywork and tyres appear to be legally correct and safe.

● That nothing is obscuring the back or front windows.

Finally, make sure you have enough fuel (petrol or diesel) for the test.

Give yourself plenty of time to get to the test centre to find a suitable parking place with ten minutes or so to spare.

Make sure you are in the waiting room about five minutes before the appointed time. Then sit and wait for your name to be called.

When you've read the number plate

correctly, the examiner will ask you to get into the car and wait for him to join you. Remember that the test has already started. Carry out the safety checks when you get in, and the starting checks before you switch on the engine.

Minor controls

Driving examiners are not only looking at the way you handle the main controls of the car – the three foot pedals, the gear lever, hand brake and steering wheel – they are also very interested to see how well you can use the minor controls.

These include the wipers and washers, the indicators, and the demister controls. Examiners often wish the candidates would do something to get rid of the misted-up windows. Make sure you know exactly how to switch these minor controls on and off; and even more importantly, that you know *when* to switch them on and off.

Similarly, you will need to keep an eye on your warning lights. Get your instructor to show you the meaning of all the lights that can come on when you are driving. These include the ignition, oil pressure, and hand brake warning lights. These should come on each time you switch on, but go off when you drive. Find out what it means if they stay on, or come on, whilst you are driving.

The emergency stop

This exercise is simply to test your reactions, and it is always the first exercise tested. The examiner will tap the windscreen with his notepad and say 'Stop'. React immediately. Hold the steering wheel firmly, and stop the car as quickly as you can without locking the wheels.

You do this by braking firmly and progres-

sively; avoid putting the clutch down until the car is almost stopped. You need to practise this exercise at various speeds and on different types of road surfaces. If

React immediately by braking firmly

the roads are very greasy you may have to brake and release and brake again in order to stop without locking the wheels.

Keeping a safe distance

The golden rule for keeping a safe distance between yourself and traffic in front is to remember the minimum braking distances in the Highway Code and to allow yourself a greater distance than is quoted.

Even if you are a good driver you must have at least two seconds between you and the vehicle in front. In bad weather you need more. So aim for two seconds plus some extra for safety.

Other vehicles

The examiner watches how you overtake, meet and cross the path of other vehicles. The main thing to remember is that one of the main causes of driving test failure is forcing any other road user to brake, swerve or take any avoiding action because of something you have done. Be extra careful when turning in front of oncoming traffic. Only overtake if you know you can do so safely. If you meet oncoming traffic in tight situations, slow down and wait if you need to.

Normal positioning of the car

The normal position of the car on the road is called a SAFETY LINE. This is the path followed when you are driving straight ahead, or turning to the left. This position is about a car door's width from the kerb, or from anything on your left-hand side.

If you are turning to the right, then you should move across the road to take up a position half a car door's width from the white line.

Where lanes are specially laid out for you, you should be in a central position in that lane.

Pedestrian crossings

Pedestrian crossings should be thought of as pieces of pavement which cross the road. As a driver you can only cross them when they are not being used by pedestrians.

Crossings come in 2 broad categories:

Controlled
These have traffic lights, or police or traffic wardens, controlling them. They are the safest sort of crossing because you know exactly when you have priority on them and when you don't.

Uncontrolled
These, such as zebra crossings, are areas

where pedestrians have absolute priority the moment they step foot on them.

Approach every pedestrian crossing feeling sure that you can stop easily and safely (after you've signalled your intentions), whenever you need to.

It is worthwhile remembering that pedestrian crossings exist at most traffic lights too. Don't stop your car on these whilst waiting at the lights.

REMEMBER

• You must accord priority to pedestrians crossing.
• You should give priority to pedestrians waiting.
• You should give an arm signal if it will help.
• You need to look out for opportunities to show that you can cope successfully with all kinds of pedestrian crossings.
• Avoid waiting on a crossing (even at traffic lights).

Stopping in a safe place

The examiner will ask you to stop on a number of occasions during the test. Sometimes he will say: 'Pull in on the left by that street lamp.' Or he might say: 'Pull up on the left at a convenient spot.' Learn to recognise the difference and know that you can choose the safest stopping place when you have to. On the other hand, do not continue driving looking for a place that really suits you. The examiner wants you to choose the most suitable spot in the immediate distance.

Check your mirrors, and give a signal if it helps; but avoid giving a left indicator if it could mislead someone into thinking that you are turning left. Brake gently, and stop at the kerbside smoothly.

Awareness and anticipation

This box on the failure sheet is filled in by the examiner for anything which doesn't really come under any of the other headings.

You can avoid being caught out by looking further ahead and planning every detail of what you are doing. Try to think in terms of what you will be doing in five seconds' time. One of the best ways to prepare for this is to give a running commentary during your lessons. As you are not likely to be very good at it yet, ask your instructor to show you how. If your instructor is not very good at it, change your instructor.

TEST YOURSELF NOW

Finally ...

Taking the test is an expensive and nerve-wracking business so don't waste time and effort by taking the test too soon. The general motoring questionnaire below will help tell you if you are ready.

Answers are listed on page 82.

1) At what age can you start to learn to drive a motor car?

a 17
b 18
c 21

2) What is the minimum distance from which you must be able to read a number plate?

a 18.5 metres
b 20.5 metres
c 27.5 metres

3) If you have applied for your first provisional driving licence, when can you start your first practical driving lessons?

a As soon as your application has been posted
b On receipt of the licence
c Only when the licence has been signed

4) When you are learning to drive, the car you are driving will need to have a current MoT test certificate if it is more than

a two years old
b three years old
c five years old

5) If you pass your test this week you may supervise another learner driver

a Immediately
b As soon as you get your full licence
c Only after at least three years

6) Seat belts need not be worn in a driving tuition car

a Whilst reversing
b For the emergency stop
c By rear seat passengers

7) The correct sequence for entering a car safely is

a Close the door, fit seat belt, adjust mirrors and then adjust the seat
b Close the door, adjust seat and mirrors, then fit seat belt
c Adjust the seat and mirrors, fit seat belt, close the door

8) The correct procedure before starting the engine is always

a Turn the key, check the handbrake and gear for neutral
b Check the gear for neutral, handbrake on, and turn the key
c Check the handbrake is on, gear for neutral, and turn the key

9) It would be illegal to drive a car if

a There was no spare tyre
b There was no water in the screen washer bottle
c There were no rear passenger seat belts

10) The most common cause of road traffic accidents is

a Road user error
b Vehicle defects
c Road design weaknesses

11) Those most at risk from road traffic accidents are in which age group?

a 3–12 years old
b 12–21 years old
c 60–70 years old

12) Braking distances increase quite dramatically as speeds get greater.
The shortest overall stopping distance at 30 mph is

a 9 metres/30 feet
b 23 metres/75 feet
c 36 metres/120 feet

13) The shortest stopping distance at 70 mph is

a 53 metres/175 feet
b 73 metres/240 feet
c 96 metres/315 feet

14) The benefit of an ABS braking system on some new cars is that it enables

a Braking distances to be increased
b Braking and steering to be done together
c Braking distances to be reduced

15) The speed limit for motor cars on a dual carriageway is

a 50 mph
b 60 mph
c 70 mph

16) The speed limit for motor cars on a single carriageway road is

a 50 mph
b 60 mph
c 70 mph

17) The speed limit for motor cars on a motorway is

a 60 mph
b 70 mph
c 80 mph

18) The sequence of approach to any hazard is

a M-S-M, P-S-L
b P-S-L, M-S-M
c M-P-S, L-A-D

19) The correct sequence for overtaking is

a M-S-M, P-S-L
b P-S-L, M-S-M
c M-P-S, L-A-D

20) It is an offence to sound the horn of a motor car

a Between 11.30 pm and 7 am
b Whilst stationary
c Inside a built-up area

21) The driver of a motor car must be covered by insurance. What is the minimum cover required by law?

a Comprehensive
b Third party, fire and theft
c Third party only

22) There is a sudden shower of rain after a long dry spell. What should you bear in

mind whilst driving?

a Reduce tyre pressures
b Tyre grip is now reduced
c Braking distances are reduced

23) You are intending to turn left at the junction ahead of you. There are pedestrians crossing the road. What should you do?

a Slow down and give way to them
b Stop and wave them across
c Sound your horn to speed them up

24) You are approaching a zebra crossing. When must you stop?

a If there is no one on the crossing
b If someone is walking towards it
c If someone has walked half way over

25) You are turning right out from a narrow one-way street into wide main road. Where should you wait safely?

a On the left near the kerb
b In the middle of the road
c On the right near the kerb

26) You are driving through a country village and you come across a shallow flood across the road. What do you do?

a Drive through quickly, keeping to the left
b Drive slowly by slipping the clutch
c Drive slowly, stopping to check your position at intervals

27) If you are the first to arrive at the scene of a road traffic accident, what should you do first?

a Move involved vehicles off the road

b Give casualties drinks to calm them
c Park your car safely

28) You are driving on a country road when you see a sign on a lamp post. It is a small circle with a black diagonal line across it. What does it mean?

a The speed limit is unrestricted
b The speed limit is 60 mph
c End of speed limit

29) Car owners must carry out regular vehicle checks. What should be checked every week?

a Brake-fluid levels
b Engine-oil condition
c Tyre pressures

30) Which of these three rules should always be followed by a courteous and safe driver?

a Never cross a double white line
b Never overtake on the left
c Watch out for young and elderly

ANSWERS TO 'TEST YOURSELF NOW'

1) a	16) b
2) b	17) b
3) c	18) a
4) b	19) b
5) c	20) b
6) a	21) c
7) b	22) b
8) c	23) a
9) b	24) c
10) a	25) c
11) b	26) b
12) b	27) c
13) c	28) b
14) b	29) c
15) c	30) c